Praise *for Pretreatment In Action*

Pretreatment In Action: Interactive Exploration from Homelessness to Housing Stabilization by Jay S Levy, MSW is a landmark accomplishment. For those who do street outreach and street medicine, Jay has provided a much-needed framework for navigating the largely undefined terrain of therapeutic relationships with people who experience unsheltered homelessness. Significantly, Jay draws on both years of direct clinical experience and a synthesis of academic, evidence-based methodologies applied to the unique world of the streets. The large underwater iceberg for many street clinicians has been the great number of persons apparently trapped in the "pre-contemplation" Stage of Change. These are the very persons who suffer and die most frequently. Jay has created the language and described the processes that can effectively guide clinicians as they engage the rough sleeping population. This workbook covers vital areas with both clarity and moral depth. His specific examples and reflective exercises are well grounded in the nuance of street work. I highly recommend this book which will undoubtedly become a cornerstone in our efforts to bring healing, hope and dignity to our sisters and brothers experiencing unsheltered homelessness.

Jim Withers, MD
Medical Director and Founder of the Street Medicine Institute
Assistant Clinical Professor of Medicine, University of Pittsburgh

I enjoyed this book very much. By using case studies and reflective exercises, Jay Levy has created a highly readable and accessible guide to working with people who are street homeless. Levy's enthusiasm for the work shines through on each page; he does not shy away from complexity, and the stories and situations he describes are as relevant in the UK as in his native USA.

This book will be invaluable for those starting out in outreach, as a practical guide to engaging those often labelled 'hard to reach'. For those of us who have been working in the field for many years it is a wonderfully refreshing read, serving as a reminder of the importance of compassion, respect, and curiosity towards those we work with. It has already influenced my practice and I look forward to buying copies for our team library.

Dr Jenny Drife
Consultant Psychiatrist
START Homeless Outreach Team for People Sleeping Rough
South London and Maudsley NHS Foundation Trust
Advisor to the Royal College of Psychiatrists on homelessness and mental health

I particularly like the style of *Pretreatment In Action: Interactive Exploration from Homelessness to Housing Stabilization*; Jay has written the book in an approachable, inviting way. It certainly is nothing like other textbooks I've read about homelessness, mental health and complex trauma! It's gentle, empathic and really focuses on the important aspect of the work — the relationship. The reader is invited in to begin reflecting their role and Jay shares his own professional experiences to help us think and learn.

Importantly, the challenges of supporting the homeless population and difficulties both in the UK, the US and elsewhere, are acknowledged here. It would be easy to bemoan the lack of adequate service provision and struggles with dominant medical/psychiatric perspectives. Instead, Jay and John Conolly, who wrote the introduction, have provided a simple summary of how easy it is for the population / community we work with to fall into the cracks, to be offered services that fit around the service but not the individual.

Getting down to the nitty-gritty, the Pretreatment approach is very hopeful and motivating. I particularly like the focus on understanding the person's inner world, sitting alongside them, sharing their terminology, gently assessing. The importance of considering safety is emphasised per Judith Herman and colleagues' complex trauma literature.

Simple summaries of guidelines, tips and hints are one of the book's defining qualities — the table in chapter 2 showing the steps of the outreach model is a revelation! Jay includes lots of tips for engagement and setting goals, hints and guides for reflective practice and his own learning experiences to support the reader's journey. We'll definitely be using this in our work.

Dr Dan Southall
Clinical Psychologist
Homeless Mental Health Team
Hull, UK

Pretreatment In Action: Interactive Exploration from Homelessness to Housing Stabilization by Jay S Levy offers a fantastic resource written from a values base of hopefulness, empowerment and compassion. Jay's commitment to enable safer and increasingly fulfilled lives for people whose lives have been about surviving not living is inspiring and motivating. The efforts made to hear the voices of those he has dedicated a career to work with and learn from creates a foundation for collaboration. As a clinician developing local services for people in Southend in Essex, UK, Jay's book will become part of my scaffold for developing nuanced and culturally sensitive provision. I found myself being inspired throughout my reading as well as the outlined narratives sparking opportunities for our own innovation. Mostly though, every sentence is written from a core of trauma informed practice. Jay's practice recognises that relationships change lives, and I'm sure the content and guidance throughout his latest book will continue to transform the worlds of so many courageous people.

Kerry Mayers, QCoP (BPS Qualification in Counselling Psychology)
Consultant Counselling Psychologist
Head of Adult Community Psychological Services in South East Essex

Five words recently uttered by an experienced street psychiatrist come to my mind after reading *Pretreatment in Action*: "the relationship is the treatment." This is not a sentimental concept, neither fluff nor idealism. It is an evidence-based counter-narrative that grounds services to people living in homelessness and enduring lives of trauma in the context of human connection rather than a traditional provider-client power imbalance. It recognizes that housing and wellbeing are only achieved and sustained in the context of trusted relationships and psychological safety.

Levy's work captures this sentiment profoundly. Marrying theory and pragmatism, Levy outlines a conceptual framework that brings meaning and structure to the work of homeless outreach and case management that is sure to help readers situate their daily work in a broader theoretical context. Lest theory remain just that, however, he incorporates numerous stories from his decades of experience that connect theory to practice and generate concrete tips for working with people experiencing homelessness.

My hope for this text is that it puts to rest harmful, stigmatizing descriptors like "service-resistant" and "non-compliant." Wherever we encounter them, the client is always on a journey of their own. The onus is on us, as it were, to meet them there every time. We don't have a silver bullet, but we do have tools and guiding principles rooted in compassion and respect. Levy's work shows us this in glistening clarity.

D. Michael Durham, MTS
Community Engagement Manager
National Health Care for the Homeless Council
Nashville, TN

Jay Levy's extensive practice, education, reflection and writing has already made a huge contribution to improve the lives of people experiencing homelessness on both sides of the Atlantic. Now his practical, "how to" guide to Pretreatment makes his work even more accessible and will therefore bring help and hope to many more. Of course, as ever with Jay's work, it is underpinned with a profound sense of shared human connections, and of healing and moral purpose.

Alex Bax, Chief Executive (London)
Pathway – transforming health services for homeless people

Clear, deceptively simple, highly practical — and timely. Jay Levy has already done more than anyone, in his earlier books, to identify and spell out the core skills of engagement with people who are homeless — often long term homeless. Now, with this new workbook, he has done it again...

Robin Johnson
Editor of *Complex Trauma and Its Effects: Perspectives on creating an environment for recovery*
PIELink Editor at http://pielink.net/

Jay S. Levy's new book, *Pretreatment In Action,* is in an interactive workbook format that engages the reader in compelling stories and exercises that integrate practice and theory. As a national (USA) trainer and author with a keen interest in Trauma Informed Care and homelessness issues, I found Jay's latest publication to be a practical tool with insightful narratives that benefit both myself and staff. Jay Levy's books need to be part of every Housing and Homeless service organization's training curriculum.

> Matt Bennett, MA, MBA
> Author of *Connecting Paradigms and Talking about Trauma & Change.*
> www.connectingparadigms.org

Jay Levy's Pretreatment approach is directed at homelessness outreach workers and their agencies. However, I will be using this book with social work students. Levy's approach is refreshingly democratic and respectful in the relating style it develops, and builds on the movement away from the worker as expert toward the worker as expert facilitator.

Levy draws on respected approaches including Motivational Interviewing, Narrative Therapy and Solution Focused Therapy. He integrates these into a clearly articulated practical approach that will also work with other significantly disadvantaged people living with trauma and marginalisation.

Engagement and relationship are the foundation of the Pretreatment approach. This is replicated in the agency commitment with workers which provides integrity and coherence across management, staff and clientele in this challenging area of work.

While Levy's work assumes the kind of resources not available in the rural context I am accustomed to, the approach will be valuable in informing the efforts of smaller communities where they unite to improve their support for those living homeless.

This guide through Levy's five pillars of the Pretreatment approach uses case studies and reflective exercises to clearly articulate and illustrate how the underlying values of respect and inclusion are operationalised. Highly recommended!

> Rohena Duncombe, BA, BSW, MSWAP
> Social work academic & researcher — Health service access for people living homeless
> Charles Sturt University, Australia

The newest edition of Jay S. Levy's work about Pretreatment and connecting people who are homeless and struggling with trauma is incredible! I can't wait until it is published, so I can share this treasure with my colleagues.

> Jane Banks, Executive Director
> South Park Inn, Hartford, CT
> www.southparkinn.org/

Jay's latest book, *Pretreatment in Action,* provides a timely reminder of the importance of understanding, connection, reflection and collaboration for homeless staff, teams, organisations and commissioners. Jay builds on years of clinical experience and previous writings, psychologically and trauma informed work and the world class Open Dialogue approach developed in Finland. In doing so, he presents guidance with a strong moral ethic of relational working, providing safety and justice doing. This book will educate those who have worked in the field for 35 days or 35 years and I highly recommend reading it, sharing it and learning from the dialogue it creates in your environment. We are all in need of the care and compassion shown in Jay's work.

Dr Colm Gallagher
Clinical Psychologist / Clinical Lead Homelessness
Mental Health and Homeless Team
Greater Manchester Mental Health NHS Foundation Trust

There's very little written about the art of homeless outreach, but here is a gift of a recipe and roadmap for hope and healing. I found Jay Levy's *Pretreatment in Action* to be a real page turner and read it in two sittings. Rather than a whodunit, it's a 'how can they' work together to find a way forward — with journeys that often begin with so much trauma and despair. The stories will stay long with you, along with the Pretreatment recipes and skills to move forward through the ups and downs and crucially use crises as opportunities.

The book and model can be easily applied to the work in the UK and the last chapter specifically relates to Psychologically Informed Environments (PIE) and working within teams and with partners, along with tips on data collection and resolving systemic conflicts. For commissioners who feel there is something wrong with a traditional emphasis on markets and metrics, this book's wisdom gives validation for the need to focus back on our humanity, learning, and relationships. The last section is particularly relevant for commissioners to appreciate what high quality staff support looks like.

A super book that I can't wait to share with outreach teams!

Victoria Aseervatham
Rough Sleeping Commissioning Manager
Westminster City Council
http://www.westminster.gov.uk/

Pretreatment In Action comes just in time for a world that realizes the need and value of equity. Building relationships is an art and meaningful engagement requires a broad palette of tools. The genius of Jay Levy's approach is that it doesn't assume that merely bearing the possibility of housing is enough or that everyone intuitively understands the nuance of human emotion and experiences. This writing offers a tangible teaching tool for social workers in the field, as well as for concerned and committed community members without assumptions as to anyone's starting point.

As someone who is an "Expert from Experience" and then came to this work wholly by accident, I can't help but imagine how much more quickly I could have moved to supporting people with this book as the spine of my practice. When reading this, imagine for a second that you are Tracy (See Tracy's Excerpt, Chapter 2), and all of the pain and challenges you would have encountered. Imagine what it would take for you to trust someone. The combination of trustworthiness and investment it would take. *Pretreatment In Action* perfectly balances the commonsense approach needed to move someone through a change process with the engagement process that ensures a continued ability to meet developing needs.

Earl Miller, MA CPS
Massachusetts Peer Recovery Network

Jay Levy's new handbook of practice addresses an issue which, to me, is central to any, medical, psychological or social intervention — the relationship between the helper and the person being helped. He presents a way to understand and develop this relationship outside a mental illness framework, but using a range of psycho-social skills and practices. The idea that one may have to engage a person in the process of developing their life for the better extends beyond the arena of homelessness and social deprivation, where it has been developed. It is equally valid and necessary in wider medical and psychiatric practice, although usually neglected in our training. And this has serious impacts. Large numbers of people do not take up, or adhere to, effective interventions, whether social, psychotherapeutic or pharmacological. There is a gap in trust between the practitioner and the client.

But what is so different here? The "therapeutic relationship" has a been phrase in common use for decades. However, it has too often been regarded as part of the "magic" of some elite practitioners, those who are recognised as being particularly effective, but no one can say exactly why. Jay manages to demonstrate not only that this issue is important, but also that it is not mysterious. There is an evidence base for it and a range of skills that can be developed. As someone who has tried to write for non-professionals for many years, I particularly like his emphasis on developing a common language, one that can help to develop understanding without raising unnecessary cultural barriers. Crucially, he provides us all with a tool with which we can improve our practice.

I am aware that this book is not primarily aimed at doctors or psychiatrists, but the importance of the skills and practices that Jay describes are essential for effective and truly client-centered practice. I, for one, will be agitating for my students and trainees to read this book.

Dr. Philip Timms, MRCS, LRCP, FRCPsych
Consultant Psychiatrist, National Psychosis Unit
Honorary Senior Lecturer, King's College London

Pretreatment In Action

Interactive Exploration from Homelessness to Housing Stabilization

Jay S. Levy, MSW

LovingHealingPress

Ann Arbor * Milton-Keynes

Learn more at www.JaySLevy.com

ISBN 978-1-61599-594-3 paperback
ISBN 978-1-61599-595-0 hardcover
ISBN 978-1-61599-596-7 eBook

Library of Congress Cataloging-in-Publication Data

Names: Levy, Jay S., 1961- author.
Title: Pretreatment in action : interactive exploration from homelessness
 to housing stabilization / Jay S. Levy, MSW.
Description: Ann Arbor : Loving Healing Press, [2021] | Includes bibliographical references and index. |
Summary: "In Levy's book, the reader will find a wonderfully crafted, detailed step-by-step manual with real-world
scenarios on how Pretreatment and the Stages of Engagement play out in the actual work of assisting the homeless.
The vignettes are rich with descriptions that clearly come from a deep repertoire of experience working in the field
that gives the reader confidence they are being guided by someone who has been in their shoes. The thoughtful
questions and space to reflect add a helpful didactic touch to the feel of the text and matches the grittiness of the
material
 being covered"-- Provided by publisher.
Identifiers: LCCN 2021027585 (print) | LCCN 2021027586 (ebook) | ISBN
 9781615995943 (paperback) | ISBN 9781615995950 (hardcover) | ISBN
 9781615995967 (kindle edition) | ISBN 9781615995967 (pdf)
Subjects: LCSH: Homeless persons--Mental health. | Homeless persons--Mental
 health services.
Classification: LCC RC451.4.H64 L48 2021 (print) | LCC RC451.4.H64
 (ebook) | DDC 362.2086/942--dc23
LC record available at https://lccn.loc.gov/2021027585
LC ebook record available at https://lccn.loc.gov/2021027586

Published by
Loving Healing Press   www.LHPress.com
5145 Pontiac Trail   info@LHPress.com
Ann Arbor, MI 48105

Tollfree 888-761-6268 (USA/CAN)
FAX 734-663-6861

Dedication

I dedicate this book to my mother, Rosalie Linksman who is 90 years young, and my wife, Louise Levy. They provide me with the meaningful connection, enduring support, and unconditional love that makes all else possible.

To all those without homes, and those who have survived homelessness, and to the Outreach workers, Nurses, Doctors, Case Managers, Experts from Experience, and others who help the most vulnerable among us. May their courage, strength and dedication serve as an inspiration to end the societal ill of homelessness.

Proceeds from this Book

The Author has pledged 25% of book royalties and other related book profits to a 501c(3) charity that supports the cause of significantly reducing and/or ending homelessness.

About Client Confidentiality

The case illustrations depicted in this book are based on actual persons and events from our field experiences. However, names, places and events have been altered as warranted to protect client confidentiality.

Contents

Foreword: The Wisdom of Pretreatment

Joel J. Hunt, MPAS, PA-C, Director, Acclaim Street Medicine
Adjunct Faculty, University of North Texas Health Science Center
Affiliate Faculty, University of Utah Family and Preventive Medicine

At first, I really did not know what I was doing, knowing only what I hoped I could achieve. Like many people who have gone into the emerging field of street medicine, my early years were full of learning a whole new culture, a new way of practicing and engaging with patients, and a lot of unlearning of outdated and/or uninformed ways to provide whole person care. Meeting people where they are both literally and figuratively is the hallmark of street medicine. This requires going to them, listening to them, and being with them; hearing their stories and listening to their struggles, their triumphs, and their souls. When I started out in Salt Lake City, Utah, I did not know that there were structures to light the path to successful transition from the streets to housing.

I fortunately had excellent guides, outreach workers and patients alike, who showed me the ropes from the basics of how to approach camps to what to do with complex social situations requiring multiple agency help. I still refer to my first patients as my teachers. There was one in particular who I think of as my street medicine professor, because he taught me that he was the director of his own health and therefore central to his own care. He was the pilot and I merely a co-pilot on his journey to achieve better health. He showed me the power differential between the traditional health care system of a brick-and-mortar clinic environment and that of meeting people on their terms, in their reality, in their space. I had the good fortune of being aware that he was schooling me on something good, on something rich and priceless in its value to my being able to work with other people sleeping rough outside, but I did not know how to put it together. Then I met Jay Levy.

It was at a National Health Care for the Homeless Conference & Policy Symposium in Washington, DC that I first met Jay and became acquainted with his work. His books were like the long lost, but familiar words I had been trying to find for years. His concepts and ease of commiserating in *Homeless Narratives & Pretreatment Pathways: From Words to Housing* connected me with a perspective I had not heard of before, yet was precisely what I had been searching for. He grounded the work of my early teachers, and transposed the knowledge they had shown me into tangible, reproducible, articulate action. This helped me to create a common language not only with the patients I was serving, but also with my team. This framework of communication and thinking helped to put the work of engagement into enough of a clinical mindset to satisfy the clinician in me and speak to the rest of the health care world, while staying true to the sanctity of the trust-building relationship with the patient. Next came the *Pretreatment Guide for Homeless Outreach & Housing First: Helping Couples, Youth, and Unaccompanied Adults,* where Jay further built on the narrative connection with patients and the Pretreatment principles. This only further nourished a quest for more guidance on the mechanics of how to do outreach, how to best practice street medicine, and how to simply *be* with patients experiencing homelessness. It also gave a structure by which to share and teach and pass on the process of working with people experiencing homelessness.

I moved from Salt Lake City to Fort Worth, Texas to help start another street medicine program. Mere months after landing in Texas, we started having street medicine interests from family medicine residents, and so we created a street medicine track. This meant formal, long-term, high level learners being introduced to Jay's books and approaches. The groundwork of the Pretreatment and Engagement Relationship Formation models have been crucial in helping residents, along with others, gain a fuller understanding and appreciation of the goals of their encounters with patients. This is an ongoing area of opportunity for improvement for everyone, and the learning never stops.

In Jay's *Pretreatment In Action: Interactive Exploration from Homelessness to Housing Stabilization,* the reader will find a wonderfully crafted, detailed step-by-step manual with real world scenarios on how Pretreatment and the Stages of Engagement play out in the actual work. The vignettes are rich with descriptions that clearly come from a deep repertoire of experience working in the field that gives the reader confidence they are being guided by someone who has been in their shoes. The thoughtful questions and space to reflect add a helpful workbook touch to the feel of the text, and matches the grittiness of the material being covered.

Pretreatment is applicable well beyond the scope of people experiencing homelessness. It has no boundaries in its usefulness. Once again, Jay deftly gives the reader the direction by which human beings can help human beings in the developmental model of the Engagement and Pretreatment process. This knows no race, creed, color, gender, or religion, but instead focuses the energy of the work on helping people to endeavor towards the goals they hope for themselves. Ultimately, I feel this is about hope. The hope that people will be able to be heard, understood, and connected. This goes for the one seeking services, as well as the one bringing services.

Pretreatment In Action: Interactive Exploration from Homelessness to Housing Stabilization is the book I wished I would have had years ago when I was beginning my journey into street medicine. I cannot overstate the importance and timeliness of this book and the insightful wisdom it has to impart.

Preface: New Beginnings

What Next?

This is the question I wrestle with at the end of every writing project. *Cross-Cultural Dialogues on Homelessness* (2018) brought together a myriad of interests and influences from both the US and UK. In all, we had five co-authors, two editors, and a great deal of support from my publisher, *LH Press*. Our research and collaboration included video conferencing, multiple emails, and exchange visits to the US and UK. Our hard work resulted in the endorsement from the UK's Faculty for Homeless and Inclusion Health, as well as adding *Cross-Cultural Dialogues on Homelessness* to the student reading list for the module on Homeless and Inclusion Health delivered at the Institute of Epidemiology and Health Care, University College London. We were grateful to receive an extremely positive book review in the US from the *Journal of Social Distress and Homelessness*[1], as well as many notes of thanks and appreciation. Most importantly, by the end of our journey we all became friends and resources for one another... our dialogue continues!

In a blink of an eye — three years have passed! During that time, multiple requests have come my way to provide more specific "hands on" guidance to applying Pretreatment Principles directly to the day-to-day challenges that staff face. This came from a variety of sources including people already working in the field of human services and those attending my in-services and trainings; a workbook for the field of Housing and Homelessness services, whether it be Health Care for the Homeless or Street Medicine doctors and nurses, or outreach counselors, shelter case managers, and Housing First staff reaching out to those in need. When I taught a graduate psychology course on outreach counseling methods, I was challenged to make my work more tangible and accessible to students with limited field experience. In return, I greatly benefited from their probing questions and their openness to new and exciting practice. The idea of creating a workbook naturally flowed from these experiences, and so, here we are.

---

[1] Matt Bennett authored the journal review entitled Shifting perspectives and finding gold: a review of *Cross-Cultural Dialogues on Homelessness*

Pretreatment In Action

I first introduced "Pretreatment" as an approach to help people without homes who experience mental health and/or addiction issues in the article, published in the *Families in Society Journal*, entitled *Homeless Outreach: On the Road to Pretreatment Alternatives* (Levy, 2000). This was the product of witnessing too many people being ignored by a treatment-biased culture that continually refused to serve those who were most in need. Inadvertently or otherwise, this approach denies the humanity of the people whom it is our mission to serve. These folks were often considered "not ready," "non-compliant," or "beyond service capabilities." In response to this dilemma, I developed a Pretreatment philosophy from an outreach perspective, which is naturally person-centered because the work begins literally and figuratively where the client is at.

My hope is to share the expertise that both providers and clients bring to their relationships. This can only take place in the midst of a true dialogue that is produced by both parties. Our main task is to create productive dialogues resulting in the co-production of goals, which serve as signposts on our journey together.

To this end, multiple exercises and questions for the reader to interact with, short excerpts, and my analysis from the field are presented for the reader to explore and consider. This provides "hands on" counsel for applying Pretreatment assessment and intervention directly to outreach and housing stabilization.

The guidance provided is especially relevant for working with folks who are least apt to raise their hands and ask for help. Many of these people are "pre-contemplative" in regard to addressing their mental health, addiction and medical needs. The question becomes not only how to become person centered, but also how to melt the "pre-contemplative iceberg" that directly contributes to their sense of "stuckness" and helplessness. This book equips us with the tools to be successful at this and much more. It's a "how-to guide" that informs our work in Homelessness Services and beyond.

Last, but not least, I thank all those who have contributed their valuable time and effort to make this workbook a reality. This includes, but is not limited to, my publisher, Victor Volkman of LH Press, for continuing to believe in the next project, Joel Hunt and John Conolly for their written contributions and feedback on this project, and of course my wife, Louise Levy, for her patience, editing prowess, and always engaging in lively dialogue about the next exciting idea. Her support and guidance are among the critical ingredients to any new project.

Introduction: Pretreatment Inclusion

John Conolly, MA, UKCP reg. Psychotherapist
Lead Counsellor, Westminster Homeless Health Service
Central London Community Healthcare NHS Trust

> "Some of the greatest tragedies of human interaction occur when an individual mis-interprets or is cut off from this language of mind and hence cannot fully grasp the many meanings of gestures of love, friendship or hostility... such a person often struggles to understand their own emotions and feels alone even when surrounded by others."
> — Linda Mayes, M.D. (2012)

"Pretreatment" is a timely reminder of just how fundamental *connection* is for people. When absent in infancy, it can lead to major psychosocial damage, which in adulthood can result in multiple social exclusion; homelessness being the tip of the iceberg. Pretreatment tunnels down to the very nitty-gritty, the nuts and bolts, of what it actually takes to *connect* with someone. This book offers the tools with which to do this. Anyone, not only in the field of homelessness, but in the field of social exclusion, will find here an invaluable toolkit with which to offer an opportunity to make good some of the paucity of connection so many homeless and excluded people have experienced on their journey in life.

Mental health experts from both sides of the Atlantic[2] see connection and communication as the medium by which our very Selves come into being. In fact, disturbance of Self in adulthood, "personality disorder," is seen as "a failure of communication... a failure of learning relationships" (Midgeley, et al., 2017, p. 23).

It is the care, communication, and connection in a stable, secure, attentive, reciprocal attachment relationship that teaches us to control, direct and share our attention with others. We only come to recognize, label, understand, and control our own emotions, as these are reflected back to us in our carers' facial and verbal expressions. Only then can we gradually come to understand our behaviour,

---

[2] USA: Jon G. Allen, Staff Psychologist, Menninger Clinic, Professor of Psychiatry, Baylor College of Medicine, Houston.

UK: Anthony W. Bateman, Consultant Psychiatrist, St Ann's Hospital, Professor, University College London; Peter Fonagy, Professor of Psychoanalysis, University College London, Chief Executive, Anna Freud Centre, London.

and other people's, in terms of mental states, thoughts, feelings, and desires; what is known in psychology as 'Mentalization,' and the basis for psychological resilience and socio-emotional maturity (Fonagy, et al., 2006; Midgeley, et al., 2017). However, this sensitive, delicate process is fragile and can be derailed in the face of neglectful parenting, trauma, stress, brought on by grinding poverty, and Adverse Childhood Events, or ACEs, meaning:

> "...notions of intrafamilial events or conditions causing chronic stress responses in the child's immediate environment. These include notions of maltreatment and deviation from societal norms" (Kelly-Erving et al., 2013, p. 721).

Homelessness is known to be the end result of a long line of trauma and to be traumatising in itself. Thus a British study (Maguire, et al., 2009) estimated that 69% of single homeless people suffer from personality disorder, 'complex trauma' or what I like to think of as 'traumatised personality' (Conolly, 2018a; Conolly, 2018b). In the UK and US, this spawned trauma informed initiatives to homelessness via the Psychologically Informed Environments (PIE) model and the expansion of Housing First.

Of course, there are socio-political, structural factors involved in homelessness, as well as a whole range of physical and mental health factors. However, Pretreatment's approach equips homelessness frontline workers to deal with what realistically is under their immediate control. That is, how to ensure that the person in front of them, who has experienced homelessness, trauma and loss, can be supported and empowered.

I remember reading Jay's *Pretreatment Guide for Homeless Outreach & Housing First* (Levy, 2013), and feeling as if an Olympic torch bearer had jumped down into the dark mineshaft I had been trying to light my way through with matches only. Here was an approach that spoke to my own experience of working with homeless people in the context of a small counselling service in central London.

It offered an approach to working with people sleeping rough that respected their journeys in life, and which genuinely wanted to understand and connect with them. It also offered, in a clear direct way, the skills and practices to do this. For me, Jay, has melded some of the fundamental principles and skills of counselling, together with his extensive experience of working with homelessness. He has extended this beyond the counselling room, and connected with people sleeping rough not only literally 'where they are at,' on the streets, but also psychologically. This is done by absolutely respecting the challenges of, and their reactions to, the journey they have endured in life, and honouring the rhythm and pace at which they can most likely tolerate and accept the help and support available. Pretreatment makes this possible by making things relevant and meaningful to even the most excluded people.

In London, my colleagues and I had been experimenting with how best to engage and connect with people who were homeless and whose circumstances were chaotic and unpredictable. This included people who failed to attend their appointments, who had taken mind altering substances, who would lose their tempers, and were convinced that counselling wouldn't help them. With the help of 'Experts by Experience' (ex-service users), and basing ourselves on Alcoholics Anonymous Groups, we had set up 'Drop-in anger support and discussion groups,' and established 'Walk-in counselling sessions.' We intuitively became much more person-centred in our counselling, more empathic, transparent, sharing our thinking, and more flexible with boundaries, like holding variable length sessions in accordance to people's attention spans, or being readily available for urgent appointments.

We also attended trainings in 'personality disorder': DBT, dialectical behaviour therapy (Linehan, 1993a; Linehan, 1993b), ST, schema therapy (Young, Klosko and Weishaar, 2003), and MBT, Mentalization Based Therapy (Bateman, Fonagy, 2006; Bateman, Fonagy, 2004)). However, although evidence based, these mainstream interventions all assumed a housed, settled population group, who were in recovery from addictions. We simply could not make such assumptions regarding our clients who were sleeping rough or had experienced extended periods of homelessness.

Pretreatment doesn't make these assumptions. Instead, it simply engages with what is, or what is presented. By basing itself on the fundamental processes of human connection, it extends the hand of inclusion and welcome into the human tribe. It is honest about where the responsibility for this lies; with the service, the workers, who, with appropriate support, are empowered to understand homeless people, their challenges, and reactions to these challenges. Counsellors are able in reflective practice to make sense of their own reactions and contributions to the cycle of misunderstanding, miscommunication and failed connection. Once they are equipped with this knowledge and language, acquired at the appropriate pace and in a non-alienating, humane manner, they can harness their clients' motivation to change in a way that is meaningful to them. This makes their accomplishments sustainable, and does not lead to the ever 'revolving door' syndrome, and chronic homelessness.

Originating in practitioner based experience over tens of thousands of hours' worth of closely observed and reflected upon experience and practice, Pretreatment is the outcome of an inductive-deductive cycle of thinking, which is why it especially spoke to the experience of my colleagues and me. Why, I believe it continues to speak to the experience of all those dedicated workers and practitioners in the field of homelessness. In the UK, Pretreatment is endorsed by the Homeless and Inclusion Health Faculty[3], and increasingly being represented in various local and national conferences[4], as well as having some input in the ongoing Royal College of Psychiatrists steering group for the Advancing Mental Health Equality (AMHE) Collaborative, which is a government funded quality improvement programme to address local mental health inequalities, including those experienced by people sleeping rough, nationally.

Jay has perceived and articulated that people only become fully human via connecting with others; at first their parents, then their peer group and colleagues. However, this process is fraught with obstacles, and can be derailed from the very first days of life. Subsequently, traumatic life events like

---

[3] *The Faculty for Homeless and Inclusion Health* published "Standards for commissioners and service providers," Version 1.0, 2011, Version 2.0, Revised September 2013, Version 3.1 October 2018 – John Conolly contributed "Standards for Counselling Services." All endorsed by various medical colleges including the: Royal College of Psychiatrists, Royal College of Physicians, Royal College of General Practitioners; the Faculty of Public Heath, the Royal Society for Public Health, University College London department of Epidemiology.

[4] Some events John Conolly presented at include: The International Homeless and Inclusion Health Conference, London, March 2013, 2014, 2015, 2016, 2018, 2019, 2020; The Postgraduate module in Homeless and Inclusion Health Multi- --Professional Panel on *Service Provider Perspectives: Working with Excluded People,* at University College London, May, 2020, 2019, 2018.

unemployment, relationship breakdown, homelessness, can expel someone from their social life-space, with all of the traumatic impact on their wellbeing, ability to function and to connect.

With Pretreatment, Jay has shown that *'Enhanced Connecting'* is *us* taking responsibility for reaching out, building and earning 'Epistemic Trust'[5] (Fonagy, 2017); jointly developing meaningful goals, with all of the support needed; us 'bridging' the diverse language cultures between services and homeless individuals; us maintaining post-referral support and transition management. All needs to be at a pace bearable for the person, who has experienced the effects of compounded trauma, undoing much of the damage and hurt.

A Pretreatment approach, with its emphasis on forming person-centered healing relationships, can alleviate many of the negative consequences that people who have been cast off to the fringes of our society have unfairly endured. Throughout his writings and practice, and once again in this offering, Jay has thrown down the gauntlet of Pretreatment inclusion. It remains to be seen whether others are willing to pick it up.

References

Bateman, A. & Fonagy, P. (2006). *Mentalization-based Treatment for Borderline Personality* Disorder: A Practical Guide. Oxford University Press.

Bateman, A. & Fonagy, P. (2004). *Psychotherapy for Borderline Personality Disorder* —mentalisation-based treatment, Oxford University Press.

Conolly, J. (2018a). "Pre-treatment Therapy: A Central London Counselling Services' Enhanced Response to Complex Needs Homelessness," Chapter 4, pp 49-69, in *Cross-Cultural Dialogues On Homelessness —From Pretreatment Strategies to Psychologically Informed Environments*, Eds, Levy, J., and Robinson, R., Loving Healing Press.

Conolly, J. (2018b). Pre-treatment Therapy Approach for Single Homeless People: The Co-Construction of Recovery/Discovery, Chapter 6, pp 109–133, in *Social Exclusion, Compound Trauma, And Recovery – Applying Psychology, Psychotherapy And PIE To Homeless And Complex Needs*, Ed Cockersell, P., Jessica Kingsley Publishers.

Fonagy, P. (2017). 'Foreword,' p x, in *Epistemic Trust and Vigilance* Midgeley, N., Ensink, K., Lindqvist, K., Malberg. & Muller, N., "Mentalization-Based Treatment For Children — A Time-Limited Approach," American Psychological Association.

Fonagy, P., Gergely, G., Jurist, E. L. & Target, M. (2006). *Affect Regulation, Mentalisation, and the Development of Self*, Karnac.

Kelly-Irving, M., Lepage, B., Dedieu, D., Bartley, M., Blane, D. & Grosclaude, P. (2013). "Adverse Childhood Experiences and premature all-cause mortality," *European Journal of Epidemiology*, Vol 28, No 9, pp 721-34. Cited by, Cuthill, F., (2019), *Homelessness, Social Exclusion And Health – Global Perspectives, Local Solutions*, Dunedin, p104.

---

[5] Child and adolescent psychologists and psychotherapists talk of *Epistemic trust*: the capacity to rely on learning, first from caregivers and then to discern who (else) to trust: *Epistemic vigilance'* To quote Peter Fonagy (2017, p. x), one of the originators of '"mentalization:" "Those who we feel respond to us — to our thoughts and feelings, not just our behavior — can probably be trusted. With those who neglect us, or misread our minds, we had better remain vigilant."

Levy, J. S. (2013). *Pretreatment guide for homeless outreach & housing first: Helping couples, youth, and unaccompanied adults.* Ann Arbor, MI: Loving Healing Press.

Linehan, M, M. (1993a). *Cognitive –Behavioral Treatment of Borderline Personality Disorder.* The Guildford Press.

Linehan, M, M. (1993b). *Skills Training Manual for Treating Borderline Personality Disorder.* The Guildford Press.

Maguire, N.J., Johnson, R., Vostanis, P., Keats, H. & Remington, R.E. (2009). *Homelessness and complex trauma: a review of the literature.* Southampton, UK, University of Southampton (Submitted). See http://eprints.soton.ac.uk/69749/

Cited in *Healthcare for Single Homeless People*, p12, Department of Health, March 2010, Office of the Chief Analyst.

Mayes, L. (2012). From her Foreword, p xi, M*inding the Child – Mentalization-Based Interventions with Children, Young People and their Families*, Eds Nick Midgley and Ioanna Vrouva,Routledge.

Midgley, N., Ensink, K., Lindqvist, K., Malberg, N. & Muller, N. (2017). *Mentalization-Based Treatment For Children — A Time-Limited Approach*, p 23, American Psychological Association.

Young, J., E., Klosko, J., S., and Weishaar, M., E. (2003). *Schema Therapy.* The Guildford Press.

Notes

The Faculty for Homeless and Inclusion Health, London, UK

The Faculty is an inclusive membership organisation for people involved in healthcare for excluded groups. Membership is open to nurses, doctors, allied medical professionals, social workers, public health experts, health advocates and support workers, commissioners, researchers and people with a lived experience of exclusion.

Its aim is to improve the quality of healthcare for homeless people and other excluded groups, by setting standards and supporting services in which generosity, kindness and compassion, combined with a passionate commitment to professional quality to become the defining characteristics of health services for homeless and multiply disadvantaged people.

1 Pretreatment Model

Introduction

This chapter presents us with an overview of the Pretreatment model to provide the reader with a general understanding and context prior to our interactive exploration of "real world" practice. A Pretreatment model is based on five universal principles of care and provides a needed compass for the complexity of our work. It is a general and flexible guide that promotes quality person-centered care without limiting creativity for both counselor and client.

What is Pretreatment? (Levy, 2010; Levy, 2000)

The term "Pretreatment" initially appeared as "Pretreatment Variables" through research that predicted successful outcomes for addiction and recovery treatment approaches (Joe, et al., 1998, p 1177; Miller & Rollnick, 1991, pp 5-29; Salloum, et al., 1998, p 35). A Psychologist, Bruce Wampold (2001) took this a step further by conducting a meta-analysis of Pretreatment variables on the success of different counseling methods for addressing mental illness. He concluded that particular therapeutic models mattered less as a predictor for success than an array of general factors such as the client's hope and expectation for change, belief in the effectiveness of the therapy, and a positive working alliance between the client and therapist.

The conclusions from research on both mental illness and addiction support the value of client-centered approaches (Rogers, 1957; Levy, 1998; Wampold, 2001), the importance of motivation and problem recognition, as well as the belief in the therapeutic model or approach by both counselor and client. Other studies on assisting people with severe mental illness uphold the effectiveness of psychosocial rehabilitation principles (Anthony, et al., 1990), which instills hope and motivation by being goal-focused. An integral part of the work is for counselor and client to jointly identify barriers to achieving one's objectives and thereby develop strategies to overcome these obstacles. This is a goal-centered approach that helps people to recognize certain concerns over time based on their aspirations, rather than the practitioner being dependent upon clients' acknowledgment of their initial problems and/or declaring themselves in need of help for psychological issues.

I have found that many people without homes who have experienced significant mental health issues including trauma often minimize their problems and/or define them differently than our accustomed treatment language. However, when engaged and supported by an outreach counselor/worker or healthcare professional, people with complex needs, inclusive of homelessness, are often open to working on goals that speak to their circumstance, which includes addressing their daily needs (e.g., food and shelter), sense of safety and future aspirations.

Most people who experience the detrimental effects of homelessness and trauma are struggling just to survive and meet their immediate needs of health and safety. The research literature (Babidge, Buhrich & Butler, 2001; Burt, et al. 1999, p. xix; Hwang, 2000; Johnson & Haigh (eds), 2012; McMillan et al. 2015; O'Connell, 2005) confirms the high risk of premature death and increased rates of chronic health issues such as arthritis, diabetes, and cancer, as well as significant rates of psychological trauma and traumatic brain injury (TBI) experienced by homeless individuals.

These conclusions from the research coupled with the persistence of a treatment-biased culture that doesn't adequately provide access for people without homes indicate the need for a Pretreatment approach. It is a relationship-driven approach based on five guiding principles of care (Levy, 2000):

- **Relationship Formation** — Establish connection and communication between worker and client. Promote trust and respect client autonomy via Stages of Engagement resulting in a client-centered relationship that is goal driven

- **Common Language Construction** — Listen, understand and utilize a person's words, ideas and values in an effort to develop effective communication

- **Ecological Considerations** — Person In Environment lens: Support the process of Transition and Adaptation to new ideas, people, housing, resources, services, and recovery, etc.

- **Promote Safety** — Apply Crisis Intervention and Harm Reduction Strategies to reduce risk, increase safety, promote stability, and embrace the opportunity for positive change

- **Facilitate Change** — Utilize Stages of Change Model and Motivational Interviewing techniques to facilitate positive change

Pretreatment (Levy, 2010) is defined as "an approach that enhances safety while promoting transition to housing (e.g., housing first options), and/or treatment alternatives through client-centered supportive interventions that develop goals and motivation to create positive change."

An outreach counseling model based on a Pretreatment philosophy affords us the opportunity to become both interpreters and bridge builders (Levy, 2013). Potential resources and services are therefore reinterpreted and reframed so the client can more fully consider these options and their potential impacts. This is the first major step toward building a bridge to needed resources and services that include housing and treatment options. It is a bridge consisting of a safe and trusting relationship between worker and client, as well as a

> Pretreatment aligns with understanding people's values and stories in a manner that imparts dignity, meaning, and purpose.

common language that fosters communication. This aligns with our efforts to understand people's values and stories in a manner that imparts dignity, meaning, and purpose to their lives.

Developing client centered relationships, understanding their worlds, and providing or accessing essential community resources and services are the mutual goals of homeless service workers (outreach counselors, street medicine practitioners, case managers, etc.) residential support staff, and their clients. In many respects the definition of Pretreatment and its five principles of care are universal and timeless.

Pillars of the Pretreatment Model

A fuller conception of the outreach counseling process that is derived from a Pretreatment approach includes ten guidelines for outreach counseling (Table 1 – p. 14) and the stages of pre-engagement through termination as represented here (Table 2 - p. 15). The Outreach Counseling Developmental Model is based upon my (Levy, 1998; Levy. 2013) synthesis of Eric Erikson's (1968) Psychosocial Developmental stages and Germain & Gitterman's (1980) Ecological phases. This includes developmental stage sensitive strategies and interventions to help guide the worker throughout the counseling process.

In closing, a Pretreatment approach embraces a dynamic set of simultaneous processes based upon five universal principles of care. These are stage-based theories of Relationship Building, Common Language Development, and Change, as well as supporting the process of transition, while always promoting and assessing for safety. These Pretreatment Principles of care provide the scaffolding, so human service workers can more effectively meet people where they are at and then proceed to develop person-centered relationships that become goal focused through ongoing dialogue. If our hope is to engage, rather than exclude the most vulnerable among us, than it is critical that a Pretreatment perspective is well integrated into our healthcare network.

The following chapters will explore specific Universal Principles of Pretreatment by engaging the reader in thoughtful excerpts from the field, questions and exercises in order to further integrate field practice and theory, so workers are prepared to help our most vulnerable clients on the journey from outreach to housing stabilization.

Table 1: Ten Guidelines for Outreach Counseling (Pretreatment Perspective)

1. Meet clients (both literally and figuratively) where they are at!

2. The relationship is most important — Promote trust and respect autonomy

3. Develop a common language of shared words, ideas and values

4. Be goal centered — Join the person in setting goals that resonate well in his or her world

5. Mutually define or characterize particular difficulties to achieving goals and jointly develop strategies or plans

6. Carefully Support transitions to new ideas, relationships (stages of engagement), environments, resources, and treatment (bridge client language to treatment language)

7. Promote Safety via Harm Reduction strategies and Crisis Intervention techniques

8. Utilize crisis as an opportunity to promote positive change

9. Respect the process of change — understand its stages and relevant interventions

10. Understand the person's narrative and integrate a person's sense of meaning or purpose with movement toward positive change

Originally published: Levy, J. S. (2011). *Homeless Outreach & Housing First: Lessons Learned*

Table 2: Outreach-Counseling Developmental Model

Ecological Phase	*Psychosocial Challenge*	Strategies & *Interventions*
Pre-Engagement Initial Phase	Trust vs. Mistrust Issues of Safety	Observation, Identify Potential Client, Respect Personal Space, Safety Assessment, Attempt Verbal & Non-Verbal Communication, Offer Essential Need Item, Listen for Client's Language, Establish Initial Communication, etc.
Engagement Initial Phase	Trust vs. Mistrust Issues of Dependency Boundary Issues	Communicate with Empathy & Authenticity, Learn Client's Language, Active Listening by Reflecting Client's Words, ideas, & Values, Identify & Reinforce Client Strengths, Provide Unconditional Regard, Avoid Power Struggles, Emphasis on Joining the Resistance, Introduction of Roles, Begin & Continue Development of Healthy Boundaries, Establish Ongoing Communication, Identify Current Life Stressors, etc.
Contracting Initial Phase	Autonomy vs. Shame Issues of Control Initiative vs. Guilt	Further Define Roles & Boundaries, Address Shame by Universalizing Human Frailty and Reviewing Client Strengths, Point Out Discrepancy & Explore Ambivalence, Negotiate Reachable Goals to Alleviate Life Stressors, Explore Client History in Relation to Goals, Determine Eligibility for Potential Resources & Services Regarding Client Interests, Further Define Shared Objectives by Utilizing Client Language, Jointly Consider Housing Options, etc.
Contract Implementation Ongoing Work Phase	Initiative vs. Guilt Issues of Stability Industry vs. Inferiority	Joint Assessment of Goals, Strengths, and Obstacles, Identify and Address Fear, shame, Guilt, and Anger Issues Through Listening, Joining, Validating and Redirect Focus to Achievable Tasks, Review & Reinforce Current Coping Strategies, Promote Self Care, Education re: Symptom Management, Further Develop Skills & Supports, Refer to Indicated Services, Enhance Coping Strategies, Mobilize Client Strengths, Support Transition and Adaptation to New Programs, Services and Housing, Reinforce Positive Change
Termination Ending Phase	Relationship Identity vs. Confusion of Roles Boundary Issues Issues of Loss	Review the Work Completed Together, Emphasize Gains, Share Feelings of Loss, Connect to Past losses, Differentiate, and Explore as Needed, Reinforce & Consolidate Change, Review & Reinforce Support Systems, Review & Redefine Provider Roles, as well as Client-Worker Relationship, Redirect to Established Support Systems

* Many of the interventions listed are applicable to different phases (stages) of the outreach-counseling process, yet have particular relevance to the indicated stage.

References

Anthony, W., Cohen, M., & Farkas, M. (1990). *Psychiatric rehabilitation*. Boston University: Center For Psychiatric Rehabilitation.

Berger, P., and Luckman, T. (1966). *The social construction of reality*. New York: Doubleday.

Babidge, N.C., Buhrich, N. & Butler, T. (2001, Feb.). Mortality among homeless people with schizophrenia in Sydney, Australia: 10-year follow-up. *Acta Psychiatrica Scandinavica*, (103)2, 105-110.

Burt, M. R. & Aron, L. Y. (2000). *America's homeless II: Populations and services*. Washington, DC: The Urban Institute.

Burt, M. R., Aron, L. Y., Douglas, T., Valente, J., Lee, E. & Iwen, B. (1999, August). Homelessness: Programs and the people they serve. *Findings of a national survey of homeless assistance: 1996 summary report*. Washington, DC: The Urban Institute.

Epston, D. & White, M. (1992). *Experience, contradiction, narrative, and imagination: Selected papers of David Epston and Michael White, 1989-1991*. Adelaide, Australia: Dulwich Centre Publications.

Erikson, E. H. (1968). *Identity: youth and crisis*. New York: Norton.

Germain, C. B. & Gitterman, A. (1980). *The life model of social work process*. New York: Columbia University Press.

Hopper, E., Bassuk, E. & Olivet, J., (2010). Shelter from the Storm: Trauma-Informed Care in Homelessness Services Settings. *The Open Health Services & Policy Journal*. 3. 80-100.

Hwang, S. W., Lebow, J. J., Bierer, M. F., O'Connell, J., Orav, E. J. & Brennan, T. A. (1998). Risk factors for deaths in homeless adults in Boston. *Archives of Internal Medicine*, 158(13): 1454-1460.

Hwang, S. W. (2000). Mortality among men using homeless shelters in Toronto, Ontario. *Journal of the American Medical Association*, 283(16): 2152-2157.

Joe, G. W., Simpson, D. D. & Broome, K. M. (1998). Effects of readiness for drug abuse treatment on client retention and assessment of process. *Addiction*, 93(8), 1177-1190.

Johnson, R. & Haigh, R., Editors. (2012). *Complex Trauma and its effects; perspectives on creating an environment for recovery* (Brighton: Pavilion)

Levy, J. S. (1998, Fall). Homeless outreach: A developmental model. Psychiatric *Rehabilitation Journal*, 22(2), 123-131.

Levy, J. S. (2000, July-Aug.). Homeless outreach: On the road to pretreatment alternatives. *Families in Society: The Journal of Contemporary Human Services*, 81(4), 360-368.

Levy, J. S. (2010). *Homeless narratives & pretreatment pathways: From words to housing*. Ann Arbor, MI: Loving Healing Press.

Levy, J. S. (2011). *Homeless outreach & housing first: Lessons learned*. Ann Arbor, MI: Loving Healing Press.

Levy, J. S. (2013). *Pretreatment guide for homeless outreach & housing first: Helping couples, youth, and unaccompanied adults*. Ann Arbor, MI: Loving Healing Press.

McMillan, T. M., Laurie, M., Oddy, M., Menzies, M., Stewart, E. & Wainman-Lefley, J. (2015). Head injury and mortality in the homeless. *Journal of Neurotrauma*. 32(2): 116-119.

Miller, W. R. & Rollnick, S. (1991). *Motivational interviewing: Preparing people to* change addictive behavior. New York: Guilford.

O'Connell, J. J. (2005). *Premature Mortality in Homeless Populations: A Review of the Literature*, 19 pages. Nashville: National Health Care for the Homeless Council, Inc.

O'Connell, J. J. & Swain, S. *Rough sleepers: A five year prospective study in Boston, 1999-2003*. Presentation, Tenth Annual Ending Homelessness Conference, Massachusetts Housing and Shelter Alliance, Waltham, MA 2005.

Prochaska, J. O. & DiClemente, C. C. (1982). Trans theoretical therapy: Toward a more integrative model of change. *Psychotherapy: Theory, Research, and Practice*. 19, 276-288.

Rogers, C. R. (1957). The necessary and sufficient conditions for therapeutic personality change. *Journal of Consulting Psychology*, 21, 95-103.

Salloum, I. M., Moss, H. B., Daley, D. C. & Cornelius, J. R. (1998). Drug use problem awareness and treatment readiness in dual diagnosis patients. *American Journal on Addictions*, 7(1).

Wampold, B. E. (2001). *The great psychotherapy Debate: Models, methods, findings*. Mahwah, New Jersey: Lawrence Erlbaum Associates.

2 Relationship Formation: The Challenges of Engagement

Introduction

Our work begins here. It is dependent on us successfully engaging with people who have experienced homelessness, multiple traumas and loss. We have learned through our dedicated efforts that engagement is the foundation of our work, while Common Language Construction is our main tool for establishing agreed upon goals and facilitating positive change (Levy, 2013).

Most counselors take the engagement process for granted, often seeing it as brief; an initial bother, or something to get through before the real work begins. The people most in need of our outreach services present us with a profound challenge of crossing many cultural divides before we can fully engage with them. This is due to our individual histories, culture, and strengths, as well as the effects of layered and compounded traumas, and the very real power differentials that people experience time and time again as they journey through homelessness.

The importance of developing a trusting relationship and our need to respect a person's individuality, culture and their need for autonomy cannot be overstated. The initial challenges of engagement are many and yet it is critical that we somehow meet folks where they are at, remain authentic in our interactions, while being conscious of our ongoing assessments and interventions. The following exercises and case excerpts, questions, and reflections will help demonstrate the critical stages of engagement.

Pre-engagement

Let's begin with our initial mindset and how this is part of the early phase of engagement, otherwise known as Pre-engagement. Our work begins before formally meeting the client. Often, we receive a referral from another agency or a concerned community member, or we meet folks who are primarily sleeping rough and/or staying in shelter via our rounds of outreach. Either way, our assessment begins as early as possible and is primarily focused on achieving a safe and welcomed

> Engagement is the foundation of our work, while common language development is our main tool.

communication between the outreach counselor and the potential client. The following two examples and exercises demonstrate the importance of our initial mindset and assessment prior to our first contact or interpersonal transaction with those in need.

Example 2-1: Phone Referral

You receive a phone call from a social service agency that states the following:

Prospective client is a Latinx Male, He is 68 years old, originally from Puerto Rico, and is primarily Spanish speaking. He has been doubling up or couch surfing with various family members and friends. His literal homeless history is limited to brief episodes of sleeping outside, before finding another family member or friend to stay with. He presents with significant and untreated mental health issues including paranoid delusions and auditory hallucinations, as well as daily alcohol use to help quell the discomfort and fear he experiences in regard to his housing instability and perceived threats from others. In the past, he has worked various jobs; his last one was in construction, which abruptly ended when he fell off a roof approximately four years ago. He currently receives retirement benefits via SSA.

Due to imminent risk of homelessness, the worker refers the client to you. The referring agency's case manager shares a sense of frustration in regard to his client being threatened with eviction from his family's residence. The client is now in a compromised position where he has no place left to go and will therefore end up homeless on the streets or in a shelter.

Questions for Consideration

Q1 Is the client eligible to receive your services? Why or why not?

_____

_____

_____

_____

_____

Here's a helpful hint: Your answer to this question is based on the type of services you provide and the eligibility criteria you apply. Consider whether the eligibility criteria help you to uphold the mission of your agency.

Q2 Regardless of whether or not the client meets eligibility standards for your services, what types of services might you recommend, or what are some potential referral pathways for getting help?

How many can you name?

_____

_____

_____

_____

_____

_____

Here's a helpful hint: Brainstorm this question based on all possibilities related to the client's description, history and situation. At this stage, do not worry about what the person is likely to accept or decline, or what specific services are available in your area.

Reflections and Possibilities

As I approach someone for the first time or when I first receive referral information, I actively begin a Pretreatment assessment. This includes considering what services and resources the person may be eligible for and *perhaps* may find useful.

During the stage of Pre-engagement, we are normally concerned about basic safety considerations for both us and the prospective client. This will be discussed at length in the next case example. The purpose of this exercise is to promote a flexible mindset that provides us with multiple opportunities, or potential pathways that we can travel once the person is further engaged and contracts for our services.

In this scenario, the prospective client may be eligible for a variety of resources and services, though much depends on what is available in any given community or service network:

Since he is over sixty years old, Elder Services ranging from Day Centers to help with housing applications inclusive of consideration for assisted or independent living settings, or priority for being an elder via Housing Authorities; Since he identifies as Puerto Rican he may benefit from Latinx services with counselors or case managers who both speak Spanish and are sensitive to Puerto Rican culture; Due to a presentation of acute mental health symptoms he could potentially gain access to Mental Health counseling services, Crisis intervention services, Respite programs or Inpatient services, as well as Department of Mental Health Case Management or Permanent Supportive Housing, or Day programs including Clubhouse Models, if his functional level and diagnosis demonstrates eligibility; Due to Alcohol Abuse issues he may benefit from Substance Abuse Services ranging from Detox to 1:1 and/or group counseling, Recovery Coach or Peer run Drop-In Centers, AA to Recovery Home settings for addiction; Due to history of falling from a roof he may have experienced a Traumatic Brain Injury so a neuro-psychological assessment may be considered, as well as the potential for Head injury or TBI services if available in your provider network; Since he has an extensive employment history he may qualify for vocational services, retraining or placement into part-time work opportunities in line with his age, current benefits and skill level; Due to his current state of literal homelessness he may be in need of a Homeless Shelter, Homelessness Resource Centers to aid in housing search, meal programs; etc.

Again, these are just possibilities and you may have come up with other options as well. Clearly, staff want to be flexible in their thinking, well engaged with the full array of community-based human services and resources, as well as understand the nuances of eligibility criteria. Developing an extensive list of resources and contacts to promote transition to services is absolutely critical to the success of our work. Whether or not we actually make the referral depends on our success via the engagement process and the person's need, want, and eligibility for these resources and services. Inevitably, we will learn more about the individual, his strengths and challenges, via the unfolding engagement process. The client and worker can then choose a referral pathway, or jointly explore new ideas and other roads to healing.

Pre-engagement Process

This example takes a look at the Pre-engagement from the standpoint of an outreach worker attempting to engage with someone in a shelter setting. The main objective of the Pre-engagement process is to achieve an initial safe and welcomed communication with the prospective client, which also implies attaining a certain level of trust and overcoming mistrust. As you read the following excerpt, consider the specific challenges of the Pre-engagement stage.

Example 2-2: Excerpt from Tracy's narrative (Levy, 1998; Levy, 2010)

A tall, black male in his mid-30s, with long, matted, black hair, mustache and beard paces the shelter floor. He has an old gray blanket with a hole in the center placed over his head and drawn over his tattered, layered clothes. He carries a small, unlit gas lantern and frequently mumbles to himself, while continuing to pace. The outreach counselor observes this potential client, and is quite surprised that he could tolerate enough structure, stimulation, and socialization to successfully gain entrance to the shelter. This person has been observed outside (sleeping rough) on several occasions, but this was his first entry into the city shelter. A glance at the shelter list reveals his name to be Tracy. Tracy doesn't talk with other guests, but continues to mumble to himself quite rapidly, and at times raises his voice with agitation. He sits down alone for small periods of time, before once again standing up and yelling, regardless of whether or not there is another person in his vicinity to receive his rage. The worker, concerned about Tracy's and others' safety, begins his evaluation of whether or not Tracy is in control of his impulses and has boundaries well enough defined to get through the night without being an imminent danger to self or others. The outreach counselor's initial assessment indicates that crisis intervention is not necessary at this time. The question is, how to get within a comfortable range for attempting an initial communication without making Tracy feel unsafe and further agitated? This exemplifies the issues of basic trust and safety that is at stake for both client and worker. The challenges of the pre-engagement stage have thus begun.

Tracy made it through the night without major incident, and was successful at not allowing anyone closer than 6-8 feet of his person. Therefore, the outreach counselor decided to walk over to the coffee pot, which was approximately 10 feet away from Tracy, getting a cup of coffee and then slowly walk back past him to the front desk. This was meant to give Tracy some familiarity with the workers' presence. One week later, Tracy's behavior seemed slightly improved, as evidenced by his sitting down for longer periods of time, as well as raising his voice less frequently. However, he still continued to mumble to himself with notable anger. Based on these improvements, the outreach counselor concluded that Tracy had shown progress in adapting to the shelter environment, and so decided to approach him and asked if he was interested in picking out some clothes. Tracy raised his voice and exclaimed, "Leave me alone!" The worker responded by attempting to make eye contact and said, "Okay, no problem," while slowly walking away. The outreach worker now realized that Tracy's clothes and/or breath smelled of alcohol, and wondered if there would be days when he might be less intoxicated and more approachable.

The counselor pondered new strategies of approach, and decided to do outreach in Tracy's general vicinity with clients who were more readily open to conversation. This would give Tracy time to adapt further to the shelter, as well as observe that the outreach counselor's interactions with others were safe and posed no initial threat. Approximately three weeks after Tracy first arrived at the shelter, the worker approached him a second time and said, "Welcome back... How are things going?" This time Tracy responded more calmly and stated, "I am a donkey who polishes the toenails of elephants!" Surprised, the counselor responded, "That sounds awfully difficult, it must be hard spending so much time on the streets and at the shelter!" Tracy looked at the counselor, half smiled and proceeded to loosely associate the topics of the jungle, the lion's den and third floor management. Although deciphering Tracy's language was a difficult task, the outreach counselor apparently had the proper ear for his first sentence. Thus began the stage of engagement!

Questions for Consideration

Q1 What were some of the Pre-engagement Strategies and/or Interventions used by the outreach counselor?

_____

_____

_____

_____

_____

_____

Here's a helpful hint: Review Table 3 (p. 25) Pre-engagement Section and consider both passive and active Strategies and/or Interventions depicted in the above excerpt.

Q2 List one or more other interventions that the worker either did or could have done to facilitate the engagement process

_____

_____

_____

_____

_____

_____

Here's a helpful hint: Reflect on what you may have tried or done when confronted with similar situations.

Reflections and Possibilities

Whenever possible we begin our initial approach to a prospective client with observation. In part, this is to assess how to engage in a safe manner such as observing the need for personal space or how the person currently interacts with others, as well as to assess the prospective client's safety and even initial eligibility for outreach services. Is the person in question in need of outreach services or are they presumed functional in attaining needed services and resources on their own or via another worker such as a shelter case manager or key worker?

An important concept to inform our early attempts of relationship formation is "desensitization," or gradual exposure to something that at first may appear threatening. Initially, this was done by the outreach counselor going over to the coffee pot near Tracy, and later doing outreach in Tracy's general vicinity with others who were more receptive, thereby modeling that interacting with him was safe.

Another pre-engagement strategy is to approach a prospective client with a need item. In this case the worker offered the option of picking out some clothes. If our initial goal is to gain entrance into the client's world, in essence to be a welcomed guest, then the idea of bearing gifts in a similar manner to visiting someone's home may resonate. Basic need items such as socks are often quite welcomed by people who experience prolonged homelessness.

Last, an essential part of pre-engagement is to manage our emotions and expectations. This includes our own sense of fear, our ability to tolerate anger, while at the same time managing boundaries in an effort to keep both the person in need and ourselves safe. If we are too cautious, then we may never choose to approach someone more than once, which was necessary with Tracy, or if we are too cavalier, we may take unnecessary risks without properly assessing the situation.

As we embark upon the Relationship formation process, including Pre-engagement, Engagement and Contracting, we should keep in mind the stage-based challenges (Table 3, p. 25) that both the worker and client will jointly experience.

Table 3: Stages of Engagement

Ecological Phase	Developmental Stage	Strategies and Interventions
Pre-Engagement	Trust vs. Mistrust Issues of Safety	Observation, Identify Potential Client, Respect Personal Space, Safety Assessment, Attempt Verbal & Non-Verbal Communication, Offer Essential Need Item, Listen for Client Language, Establish Initial Communication, etc.
Engagement	Trust vs. Mistrust Issues of Dependency Boundary Issues	Communicate with Empathy & Authenticity, Learn Client's Language, Active Listening by Reflecting Client's Words, Ideas, and Values, Identify & Reinforce Client Strengths, Provide Unconditional Regard, Avoid Power Struggles, Emphasis on Joining the Resistance, Introduction of Roles, Begin & Continue Development of Healthy Boundaries, Establish On-going Communication, Identify Current Life Stressors, etc.
Contracting	Autonomy vs. Shame Issues of Control Initiative vs. Guilt	Further Define Roles & Boundaries, Address Shame by Universalizing Human Frailty and Reviewing Client Strengths, Negotiate Reachable Goals to Alleviate Life Stressors, Explore Client History in Relation to Goals, Determine Eligibility for Potential Resources & Services Regarding Client Interests, Further Define Shared Objectives by Utilizing Client Language, Review & Reinforce Current Coping Strategies, Jointly Consider Housing Options, etc.

Many of the interventions listed are applicable to various phases (stages) of the outreach process, yet have particular relevance to the indicated phase. Concepts from Germain and Gitterman's (1980) Life Model and Eric Erikson's (1968) Psychosocial Developmental Model influenced the formation of the above table.

Engagement Phase

As indicated in table 3, the engagement stage is centered on developing trust between the worker and prospective client, as well as establishing the boundaries of an outreach counseling relationship. The main goal of this stage is to achieve welcomed ongoing communication in an effort to set the table for contracting or a mutual agreement to work on acceptable goals between worker and client.

This example takes a look at the Engagement process between the outreach counselor and prospective client — Tracy. We join them in the midst of their journey toward a productive dialogue.

Excerpt from Tracy's Narrative (Levy, 1998, Levy, 2010) — Part 2

After their initial communication, Tracy and the outreach counselor continued to talk with each other on a weekly basis. During these early meetings, the counselor would often clarify his role as an outreach worker who could provide services ranging from applying for benefits or affordable housing to just being there as a supportive presence. However, there were times when Tracy was quite intoxicated and would express extreme anger, as evidenced by verbally abusing others within his general vicinity. When such abuse was directed toward the worker, he would intervene by stating, "I hope we can talk again when things are calmer," and then walk away. At first this made it difficult for the outreach counselor to approach Tracy again, dreading the possibility of further verbal abuse, but this never became a fixed ongoing pattern.

Over the next four to five weeks, they discussed issues ranging from the condition of Tracy's feet to repeated communications about the jungle, the lion's den, and problems about third floor management. After hearing these terms in various contexts, a sense of meaning formed, which was consistent with Tracy's responses. The jungle appeared to be his way of referring to life's struggles, and the lion's den was apparently a biblical analogy to the shelter and or/streets being full of dangers. Finally, third floor management seemed to mean the bureaucracy with all its flaws and difficulties.

The outreach counselor and Tracy were now able to communicate through this sense of metaphor and talked about ways to escape the lion's den, as well as how to better deal with the jungle by not getting caught up in third floor management. In other terms, how to leave the shelter, while successfully coping with life's challenges and cutting through the red tape of bureaucratic systems. Further, the outreach counselor was able to compliment Tracy's strengths in ways that he could more readily hear. For instance, the counselor said, "I admire your courage when dealing with the jungle and returning to the lion's den on a regular basis. It will take the same kind of courage to eventually leave this place for something better." This became the theme of many conversations, although often Tracy's loose associations were much too confusing for the counselor to follow and appeared quite unrelated to matters at hand. Whenever this happened, the worker made a bridge back to the here and now. For example, Tracy once perseverated for ten minutes on aliens visiting other worlds. The worker found a slight pause in the conversation and quickly interjected, "Tracy, just like the aliens entered new and uncharted territories, you did the same when you first came to the shelter. This has got me wondering... what is the shelter like for you... how have you managed to get along here?" This intervention was quite successful at helping Tracy to refocus on issues that he and the counselor could jointly discuss, thereby promoting the engagement process for both of them. In a very real sense, they had learned each other's language and their worlds were no longer alien. Trust between Tracy and the outreach worker had formed on an interpersonal level and future possibilities now included contracting.

Questions for Consideration

Q1 What does Tracy value?

_____

_____

_____

_____

Here's a helpful hint: Consider what makes Tracy uncomfortable or what he does not like as this may shine a light on what he values. What Tracy values may provide an excellent way to keep communication open.

Q2 How can we learn more about Tracy's wants/needs and interests?

_____

_____

_____

_____

Here's a helpful hint: Explore this more globally than simply asking him this question… How do we set the table for our words to resonate, so that inviting Tracy to share information can help us help him?

Q3 What were some of the Engagement Strategies and/or Interventions used by the outreach counselor? (refer to Table 3, p. 25)

_____

_____

_____

_____

_____

Here's a helpful hint: Consider both passive and active Strategies and/or Interventions

Reflections and Possibilities

"What does Tracy value?" is a question that we will answer again and again as we get to know Tracy and his narrative. Over time his words, ideas, and values will become more known to us, if we are successful in fostering ongoing communication. For now, we have limited information, though he has made some things clear in regard to what he dislikes.

What we do know is that Tracy is prone to drinking alcohol, so perhaps we can say that under certain circumstances he values drinking. We often see this in the homeless world as an addiction, but also as a way of coping… perhaps making oneself numb to the trauma or even physical pain of homelessness or to help dampen certain symptoms of mental illness such as anxiety or hearing unwelcomed "voices" (auditory hallucinations). He has also shown some agitation in regard to being approached by others, so we may surmise that he values his privacy, autonomy and safety. These are basic sensibilities that most of the folks that we meet feel strongly about… maybe more so than comfortably housed and high functioning individuals who may take some of these things for granted. So, there is a sensitivity, in part due to trauma and loss, when these basic "rights" appear to be threatened by others.

The way we learn more about Tracy's needs, wants and interests is by advancing the engagement process and gaining a better understanding of Tracy's language or meaning intended by his communications, as well as gaining a fuller appreciation of his life story. In essence, we need to build strong communication based on a common language of reference, so we can better appreciate Tracy's needs, wants, interests, and values. Our hope is to have his strongly held preferences directly reflected upon during the goal setting or contracting stage that follows engagement. This aspect of our work will be discussed in greater detail in the next chapter, which focuses on "Common Language Construction" and "narrative approaches" to our work. For now, we should note that Tracy has been responsive to questions about the condition of his feet (he values healthy feet), and has on more than one occasion brought up the terms "The lion's den," "the jungle," and "third floor management," so it is important to develop a greater sense of what he means by these terms and how they *may* connect with his life experiences and future goals.

The outreach counselor used a number of strategies and interventions to promote engagement. This included the critical step of introducing and broadly defining one's role as an outreach worker, as well as working on the development of informal yet professional boundaries within an outreach context.

Initially, the outreach counselor was challenged due to Tracy's level of intoxication and expression of anger toward people in his vicinity. This made it difficult for the worker to approach him, but given enough time and familiarity an initial communication via the Pre-engagement process was established. During early engagement the worker began more frequent interactions with Tracy. When Tracy presented with gross intoxication, some heightened expressions of agitation were directed toward the worker. In response, a boundary or limit was set by stating to Tracy, "I hope we can talk again, when things are calmer," before slowly walking away. The counselor's intervention of walking away while leaving communication open seemed effective at stopping the abusive behaviors from escalating, thereby preserving the engagement process. Their informal meetings often focused on the here and now, such as whether Tracy needed socks or the condition of his feet. This also included tuning into Tracy's words and reflecting them back to show understanding and connection. The counselor even utilized Tracy's terms such as the "lion's den," "jungle," and "third floor management" to reflect on Tracy's courage and thereby provide positive regard. Lastly, there were times when the worker needed to set a boundary on Tracy's tangential or loosely associated speech. This was done with much empathy and patience by waiting for a momentary pause in the conversation, and then redirecting him back to the here and now.

As depicted in Table 3, the worker attempted to establish trust while developing the boundaries of their working relationship. Direct interventions included ongoing outreach to Tracy, defining roles and boundaries, communications that showed empathy paired with offering need items such as clothes or socks, active listening and reflection of Tracy's words and ideas (understanding and utilizing client language), avoidance of power struggles, etc. This resulted in achieving an ongoing welcomed communication with Tracy, as well as the development of some common references to begin the productive dialogue of setting mutually acceptable goals.

Contracting Phase

The objective of the contracting stage (phase) of the engagement process is to set mutual goals that resonate well within the client's frame of reference (use of common language) and is consistent with the counselor's work role. It is critical to build on the trust established during the Engagement phase, as well as to respect client autonomy to self-determine the parameters and pace of our work. We now re-join

Tracy and the outreach counselor to observe and better understand the process of contracting for services.

Excerpt from Tracy's Narrative (Levy,1998; Levy, 2010) – Part 3

Tracy now showed greater interpersonal relatedness and was quite lucid for up to fifteen minutes at a time, before becoming tangential and perseverating on matters beyond the worker's scope. When arriving at the shelter, Tracy was often intoxicated, but the counselor continued to meet with him unless he was extremely drunk. When Tracy appeared to be too intoxicated to hold a productive conversation, the outreach worker waited to the next meeting and stated, "Tracy, when you drink a great deal, it is difficult for us to understand each other. I value our conversations and you appear to be in better control of yourself and surroundings when not drinking." If Tracy objected to these ideas, the relationship was now strong enough for the counselor to give a description of how upset and angry Tracy becomes when intoxicated and how this could make him and others less safe. Tracy values "safety," so this theme was successfully utilized during their many conversations.

Over time, Tracy gradually shared some of his housing, educational and psychiatric history. He reported attending one year of college before having great "difficulties." He has a history of psychiatric hospitalization that included being prescribed neuroleptic medications. The outreach counselor slowly explored the nature of Tracy's perceived "difficulties" at college, as well as in the here and now. Further, the worker inquired as to how Tracy felt about his past experiences on neuroleptic medications. Tracy clearly stated that he was not interested in medications. The worker made a mental note of this, and in time would attempt to educate him on the wide variety of psychotropic medications now available, thereby reframing their possible application. All of this information was gathered bit by bit, and when paired with Tracy's mental status it became evident that he was eligible for Department of Mental Health (DMH) services inclusive of transitional housing.

The terminology that Tracy often used still consisted of "the lion's den," the "jungle," and "third floor management." The utilization of these terms between Tracy and the worker improved their communication. The role of the outreach counselor was now defined with greater clarity as a social worker connected to community resources that Tracy could consider. The counselor thought that the time was right, so he approached Tracy and said, "We've talked a lot about the shelter being a lion's den, and the streets a jungle, therefore would you be interested in the goal of finding a safe place to live?" Tracy responded immediately, exclaiming, "I've tried this before and always got caught up in third floor management!" This was followed by Tracy making several unclear statements with escalating anger. Although the worker could not make out exactly what he was saying, it provided valuable insight about Tracy's plight. It was now clear that he had a history of some bad experiences via DMH housing or the mental health system.

They re-engaged over the next week and talked about less charged issues. During this time, Tracy expressed some new difficulties around the condition of his feet, which had become increasingly blistered and in need of medical care. The counselor asked Tracy if he would like to meet the nurse and

Tracy agreed. Subsequently, the shelter nurse began giving him foot soaks. This was the first contract for services between the worker and Tracy, which led to immediate implementation.

After several foot soaks, the outreach counselor once again approached Tracy and said, "I am glad to see that your feet are better! Are there any other goals that you would like to work toward?" Tracy once again spoke of the lion's den, and wondered if there was a way out. The worker immediately responded, "I know of a smaller transitional living space (transitional residence for adults with mental illness) with good people who are safe and trustworthy" and then asked how Tracy felt about hearing this. Tracy began to show some interest, as evidenced by him softly biting his lip and not responding immediately. This time the worker reinforced that the transitional residence was "safe," and that he would not have to go through a great deal of "third floor management." Tracy then asked, "Where is this transitional residence located?" After five months of outreach, they had firmly entered the stage of contracting and set up an initial objective to consider living space alternatives to the generic shelter.

Questions for Consideration

Q1 What were some of the Contracting Strategies and/or Interventions used by the outreach counselor?

_____

_____

_____

_____

_____

Here's a helpful hint: Review Table 3 (p. 25) Strategies and Interventions section under the Contracting Phase, while keeping in mind that some of these strategies overlap with the other stages of the engagement process and are built upon from there.

Q2 What are some of the pitfalls or potential barriers to successfully progressing through the contracting stage?

———

———

———

———

———

Here's a helpful hint: Instead of the knee-jerk tendency to identify reasons why the client may not be ready to engage further, think about barriers that are transactional in nature between the outreach worker and client. Consider, what was the value of offering foot soaks, after Tracy's apparent rejection of the idea of housing?

Q3 Why do you think the engagement process, inclusive of the contracting phase, is longer for some people and shorter for others?

———

———

———

———

———

Here's a helpful hint: Review table 3 (p. 25) and consider your own experiences of working with clients where it took a great amount of outreach, time, and patience to establish agreed upon goals versus those where it was a relatively quick process.

Reflections and Possibilities

The outreach counselor began the contracting stage by continuing outreach and reinforcing boundaries. A limit on when it was "safe" for them to meet was now reinforced through conversation with Tracy when he was relatively sober. Instead of just avoiding Tracy during his times of gross intoxication and anger, or walking away if he became verbally abusive, it was reframed as a request by the outreach counselor. The outreach worker shared with Tracy that he enjoyed their meetings and conversations, though sometimes when he was inebriated things would break down or become much more difficult. It was an important step to make this part of their ongoing dialogue, as significant intoxication paired with angry verbal outbursts may become a barrier to reaching future goals as well. In motivational interviewing terms, the worker pointed out a discrepancy in regard to Tracy's want or need to speak with the worker and his occasional heavy intake of alcohol resulting in angry outbursts. This intervention was only successful because the worker and Tracy had first established trust, so Tracy now valued their relationship. The timing of this type of intervention was critical to its success.

The first or initial contract for services was in regard to the worker offering Tracy a foot soak via the Health Care for the Homeless Nurse. Tracy directly brought up a concern about his feet and the worker responded accordingly. This was effective because the counselor responded directly to what Tracy wanted. In this sense Tracy owned the process, rather than the worker trying to take control with a different agenda.

The dialogue between Tracy and the outreach counselor had expanded significantly over time. Tracy now shared a bit of his history and they established an acceptable communication utilizing the terms "Being Safe" or "Safety," "Lion's Den," the "Jungle," and "Third Floor management." The technique of developing a common language between worker and client will be discussed in detail during the next chapter. For now, it is important to recognize how the worker used these terms to eventually frame out the offering of transitional housing, so it could resonate in Tracy's world. The first attempt was rejected by Tracy stating in an angry tone that he had tried getting housed before and it always got caught up in third floor management. The outreach counselor followed Tracy's lead and did not press the issue until after the initial success of helping him to attain a foot soak. Often, success with smaller, more attainable goals can help to further build trust and confidence in the working relationship resulting in some gumption, or even initiative toward taking larger steps.

In regard to pitfalls or barriers to successfully contracting with clients, it helps to be centered on the transactional nature of the helping relationship. Our initial premise is that a person in need is almost always ready for assistance as long that it is offered in a way that resonates well. Therefore, the onus is clearly on the counselor to get where the client is at. In other words, we, the counselors, outreach workers, and case managers are the ones who are often "not ready" for the client.

This is why stage-based theories are so helpful. They give us guidance to remain where the person is at. One major pitfall or barrier to successfully completing the Contracting stage of engagement is making wrong assumptions about where the client is at. We must continually assess whether or not the client has entered the Contracting Stage, as well as re-assessing whether or not they remain in that stage during our stage-based interventions. Assessment is fluid... it is an ongoing process throughout our work. The stages of engagement are not linear in the sense that the client always progresses from pre-engagement to engagement, and then to contracting. They can at any point regress to an earlier stage due to some new input, or their own type of assessment that turns them away from the relationship. Many things can trigger a client to mistrust the worker and/or the process of moving forward through the contracting stage, so that goal-driven work can begin.

The question becomes how to promote the growth of the relationship by building trust and respecting client autonomy to instill a sense of motivation and initiative toward positive change. In order for this to be successful, worker needs to start with limited expectations and has a certain comfort level with not knowing how things will unfold. If a worker tries to control the process and move it in the direction that they want, then the individuality, expertise and/or the strengths of the client are no longer front and center. If the autonomy of the client is not properly respected, this can lead to a sense of shame for not being good enough, guilt for not pleasing the worker, or an unhealthy dependence of needing the worker to control things, or even a sense of fear of being controlled and having one's sense of freedom stripped away. These are all powerful feelings that are often hidden behind anger and rage when we get a "fight" response, or silence and avoidance when we get a "flight" response from the person in need.

These natural tensions to the development of a helping relationship are informed by Eric Erickson's (1968) Stages of psychosocial development as applied to relationships. The pivotal developmental conflicts to relationship formation are depicted via table 3 as Trust vs. Mistrust; Autonomy vs. Shame; Initiative vs. Guilt.

We do meet some folks in need who readily engage with our services and are immediately ready and wanting to discuss their goals. The particular outreach services that I manage provide only short-term work with such persons as we are able to quickly refer and redirect them to the community-based resources and services that they desire and need. At most, this takes a meeting or two to assess and refer appropriately. These are the folks who are already raising their hands and requesting services. For them, our lengthy view and exploration of the engagement process seems less necessary.

Outreach services are designed to reach the people who are not raising their hands, but are in dire need of help. Many of these folks are pre-contemplative in regard to at least some of their mental health, addiction, or medical issues. Within this subgroup there is a wide range of responses to the engagement process. With some folks this can still be a relatively quick process involving multiple contacts over a week or two, while with others this can take many months to achieve.

There are a variety of factors that impact the length of the engagement process. Some of these were discussed earlier, but it is worth exploring further. Partly it has to do with the degree of trauma experienced or the complexity of issues many of our clients face, ranging from poverty and homelessness to significant loss, addiction, severe mental illness, and major medical concerns. A person's history with relationships including negative experiences with past human service workers comes into play. Similarly for the worker, our history with past relationships and our own issues can cloud the picture, as well as our own counter-transference reactions to perhaps try and "save" people. This may lead to inappropriate risks, or it becoming an all too personal endeavor for the counselor. If the client does not respond how we had hoped, it inevitably leads to disappointment and frustration. Another common dynamic is for the counselor to be too cautious due to an exaggerated fear of the current situation or a discomfort with the client's angry responses. All of these things can lead to unwise interventions or avoidance of folks who are clearly workable. As mentioned earlier, our own need for control and/or not being emotionally centered enough to allow the work to unfold without meeting our expectations is another element that impacts the length of the engagement and contracting stages.

Finally, and perhaps most importantly, we must understand that in approaching each new client in need, often we must cross several cultural divides for our work to be successful. Depending on the identities of the worker and client, this can be numerous, or small in number.

Here are some of the cultural divides that may be in need of crossing. These include socio-economic (different income levels), as well as difference in culture, race, and ethnicity, age, gender, LGBTQ status, and so on.

In regards to staffing, it is very helpful to hire diverse staff, as well as peers or experts by experience, so they can be matched to clients in a manner that reduces the number of cultural divides between them. We must also encourage an open dialogue in regard to considering and exploring the diverse perspectives these differences generate, as well as the resulting barriers to care (personal, institutional and structural) when discussing outreach and engagement strategies during 1:1 and group supervision or co-vision. A Pretreatment approach can be particularly helpful toward crossing these divides.

In the end, tapping into trusting relationships and their power to heal is the key to successful outreach and recovery. The hope is to transition from an "us and them" to a "we." This joining process, that of crossing cultural divides in an effort to engage vulnerable people in productive dialogue, will be demonstrated and discussed in detail during the proceeding chapters. The person-centered relationship building process is the very foundation of our work. Pretreatment's five principles of care guide us toward this noble objective. The next chapter will add an essential layer to the relationship-formation process by reviewing how to foster better communication through a common language, which is an essential component to our success at reaching those who are excluded and continue to struggle with complex trauma and multiple needs.

References:

Erikson, E. H. (1968). *Identity: youth and crisis.* New York: Norton.

Germain, C. B. & Gitterman, A. (1980). *The life model of social work process.* New York: Columbia University Press.

Levy, J. S. (1998, Fall). Homeless outreach: A developmental model. *Psychiatric Rehabilitation Journal,* 22(2), 123-131.

Levy, J. S. (2010). *Homeless narratives & pretreatment pathways: From words to housing.* Ann Arbor, MI: Loving Healing Press.

Levy, J. S. (2013). *Pretreatment guide for homeless outreach & housing first: Helping couples, youth, and unaccompanied adults.* Ann Arbor, MI: Loving Healing Press

3 Common Language Construction: Entering the House of Language

Introduction

A Pretreatment approach focuses on getting person-centered with potential clients who, for a number of reasons, inclusive of significant trauma history, difficulties trusting others, denial of significant clinical issues, and the inflexibility of treatment-biased services, are among the most disaffiliated from our healthcare network. It is very easy to deem people who are pre-contemplative in regard to accepting clinically defined diagnoses or formalized treatment protocols as "not ready" to participate in our services, thereby relieving ourselves of any obligation. However, when it comes to outreach counseling and street medicine, this IS the "challenge to care."

As an outreach counselor, supervisor, and program manager, I have witnessed on countless occasions how all this can change once we establish a trusting relationship that clearly respects a person's autonomy, as well as positive communication based on mutually accepted words, ideas, and values to guide our working relationship. Ultimately, the goals, even if initially thought of as clinical in nature, need to be defined through the client's language. I am fond of saying that the engagement process sets the foundation of our work, while utilizing a Common Language is our main tool for getting it done. Both are necessary to achieve a goal-driven person-centered relationship.

Our objective is to enter the same house of language as the client, or at least be invited to play on the "mutual playground of language" that is located between the worker's and client's houses. Everything begins with the worker listening for the words, ideas, and values of the client and then reflecting back what is heard to make sure we are developing a keen sense of what is being communicated.

The following exercises, excerpts and questions for the reader bring to life the challenges of the Pretreatment principle of Common Language Construction and its critical importance in upholding the sanctity of the helping relationship.

Exercise 3-1 will help us appreciate the challenge of perception. Our initial task is to do our best to take in the full picture and/or meaning behind what is being said. Let's begin with a visual illustration.

Exercise 3-1: Gestalt Psychology Figure

Take a look at the figure at right (Hill, 1915; Boring, 1930)

Describe what you see

_____

_____

_____

_____

Discussion

This is a reversible figure, so many viewers will see either a Young Woman or an Old Lady. While it is virtually impossible to see both at once, it is possible to switch your focal point within the field of view causing a different gestalt to materialize, and thereby transform the Old Lady to a Young Woman or visa/versa. In this figure, the Young Woman's jaw and chin becomes the Old Lady's nose, or the Old Lady's mouth becomes the Young Woman's necklace.

Gestalt Psychology (Perls, 1969) teaches us that changes in our focus (focal point) in relation to the field (ground) can lead to drastically different interpretations of the visual data (ground + focal Point = Gestalt). Now let's think about this in regard to our experiences and perceptions of a person's words and ideas (auditory data) within the context of our work.

Exercise 3-2: Our Work Focus

Take a moment to reflect on a particular work assessment (e.g., intake form) you currently utilize with clients. At what point in your work do you use this assessment?

Does it provide an important and distinct focus to guide both your questions and how to interpret the client's answers? Think about how this impacts your focus... what do you tune into and what do you miss out on?

_____

_____

Discussion

Throughout our work we use a variety of assessments to both guide our interventions and better understand the people we serve. Ironically, the more specificity the assessment provides, the more it may blind us to a fuller presentation of the person that encompasses their interests, values, culture, life experiences, multiple strengths, and aspirations, as well as their deficits, challenges, functional level, trauma, and diagnoses, etc. Most of all, our assessments tend to divorce us from the person's story and instead objectifies our clients through quantitative measurements, rather than qualitative analysis. This is not meant to devalue our assessments, but rather to remind us that they present a limited picture, rather than the whole story.

We began with an exercise that featured a reversible figure (Old Lady/Young Woman) demonstrating some basic ideas from Gestalt Psychology (focal point + ground = gestalt). When looking at this picture, we tune into either the Young Lady or the Old Woman, as opposed to seeing both simultaneously. Similarly, our assessments will limit our perspective on the whole, while enriching our thought process and interventions in regard to very specific concerns. For example, if our assessment is problem and/or deficit focused in order to ferret out symptom complexes for the purpose of diagnosis, then it will certainly be blinded to a person's values, strengths, and aspirations. This is akin to just seeing a small part of the overall picture, or having a very limited understanding of a person's story.

In comparison, a Pretreatment assessment takes place within the context of the person's narrative and depends on its five guiding principles of care. Our focus is on getting person-centered, which demands that we tune into the person's story. This cannot be effectively done without first committing to the process of "Common Language Construction." Otherwise, we will be viewing the person and our work through an overly restricted lens. The greater our understanding of people within the context of their narratives, the more we can work with, rather than inadvertently working against their values, aspirations, and sense of meaning. Our hope is to widen the field of view before narrowing our focus to mutually defined goals.

Fostering Communication

The main objective of Pretreatment is the formation of a person-centered relationship that is goal-focused. The key to success is rooted in our striving to develop a common language between outreach counselors and vulnerable, hard-to-reach people. Whether it is engaging with an individual client, referring people to potential resources and services via social agencies, or advocating for change in governing policies, our mission is to find an effective means to cross many cultural divides. Our task is to become interpreters and bridge builders across systems of care. The main tool for achieving this is the development of effective communication, which is based on the art of common language construction.

We are immersed in language, yet challenged on how to communicate well with others. Friedman and Combs (1996, p. 29) state, "Speaking isn't neutral or passive. Every time we speak, we bring forth a reality. Each time we share words, we give legitimacy to the distinctions that those words bring forth." Berger and Luckman (1966) describe language as our pathway toward knowing what is real in everyday life, influencing our social interactions, and the formation of our inner worlds. There is a power in words to transform our reality. In this sense, language creates the world in which we communicate and live.

Heidegger declares (1971, pp. 63 & 135), "Language is the house of being." It is through language that we define our relationships with ourselves, others, and the world around us. Each person we meet, as well as the services, resources and programs we attempt to access, resides in its own "house of language." It is a house built upon the words, ideas, and values that are critical to one's sense of self, purpose, or the mission a particular program or service sets out to achieve.

Common Language Construction is an essential process to crossing cultural divides. It builds bridges between the many "houses of language" we encounter in our daily work. Our objective is to foster communication with both the people we serve and the referral resources that are essential to their well-being. Our charge, as outreach counselors, case managers, and health care providers, is to facilitate productive dialogue on all levels.

Let's further explore the linguistic aspects of our work via Miguel's narrative as depicted in the next example. Try to cue into the cultural divides between the worker and potential client, as well as culturally sensitive interventions and strategies utilized to enhance communication in an effort to better understand Miguel's world.

> **Our task is to become interpreters and bridge builders across systems of care.**

Example 3-1: Excerpt from Miguel's narrative (Levy, 2018)

I (white, male, Outreach Counselor in his mid-30s) first met with a sixty-four-year-old Latino male named Miguel at the Boston Common during the early spring of 1996. I approached Miguel because he was shoeless and carrying a blanket. I responded to what appeared to be his immediate needs by offering socks and asking if he'd like us to go shopping for footwear.

At first, Miguel proudly declared the toughness of his feet. He then informed me of his childhood history of walking barefoot along the roads, rocks and sands of Puerto Rico. I quickly agreed with his assessment, but then gently pointed out that getting something for his feet would simply provide the choice of when to go barefoot. In the end, Miguel was very appreciative and agreed to my offer. Together we purchased the sandals he preferred, as opposed to sneakers or shoes.

The process of engagement was off to a good start and Miguel shared with me details of his impoverished childhood, yet strong community bonds, followed by the slow unraveling of family ties after his move to the mainland. He connected his current difficulties as related to ageism, cursed his isolation from others, and in many ways felt driven to drink. Our strong connection was further confirmed when he later showed me his bottle of rum and offered me a "hit," which I politely declined. This was the beginning of our journey. Many outreach meetings soon followed.

Miguel very much wanted to be placed in housing and to become part of a community, but often felt disrespected and left out. In contrast, our relationship helped to bring him a sense of connection. Together, we agreed to search for an affordable place to live. Miguel had a steady income through Social Security benefits, and he was eligible for elder housing. This was a great opportunity, because the wait for subsidized housing in Boston was several years unless the applicant was able to document priority status as an elder or Veteran. This reduced the waiting time from years to just a few months.

However, this was tricky because Miguel did not consider himself to be an elder and really despised the term. He believed that being an "elder" meant that you were feeble, weak, and cast aside by others. I quickly learned that any mention of the term brought about an angry response. In this manner, the words we use and their perceived, not necessarily intended, meanings can have major ramifications.

Questions for consideration

Q1 What are the cultural divides between the outreach counselor and Miguel?

_____

_____

_____

_____

_____

Here's a helpful hint: Think broadly about the term "cultural divide" as identifying an array of differences between two people, not just differences in ethnicity.

Q2 What type of engagement strategies were used to help cross these cultural divides?

———————————————————————————————————

———————————————————————————————————

———————————————————————————————————

———————————————————————————————————

———————————————————————————————————

   Here's a helpful hint: Consider both pre-engagement engagement interventions (See table 3, p. 25) and also focus on the outreach worker's specific questions and how they were received by Miguel.

Q3 The use of the term "elder" was initially rejected by Miguel. Why? How does this reveal Miguel's values? What possibilities are opened up by this realization?

———————————————————————————————————

———————————————————————————————————

———————————————————————————————————

———————————————————————————————————

Reflections and Possibilities

   Our success in reaching out to disaffiliated persons with complex needs is dependent upon our ability to respond to their immediate needs, daily concerns, and future aspirations. This also demands that the counselor has an awareness of cultural divides and other potential barriers to the engagement process.

   In this case, the worker (W, M, Mid-30s) is significantly younger than Miguel (L, M, 60s), and of a different ethnicity and race. As we attempt to engage our clients, we need to be aware of the many cultural divides that may exist in regard to race, ethnicity, age, gender, LGBTQ identity, place of origin, socio-economic status, religion, as well as social-cultural connections, overall life experience, etc.

The counselor begins his outreach by approaching Miguel and offering a need item that often resonates well among persons who are sleeping rough. Many of these folks lack access to clean clothes and may experience difficulty keeping their feet clean and dry, which puts them at risk for infection and/or trench foot. There is an old (anonymous) adage among outreach workers that states, "If you want to get to someone's head, begin with their feet." So here, the offering of socks and footwear serves a dual purpose of promoting engagement and health. The counselor's offering a need item can also be viewed as a way to establish peaceful intent, or a "gift" that one might bring when visiting a friend's house or living space. It can help establish a safe presence, thereby reducing the immediate impact cultural divides may present, while setting the table for further engagement.

Early on, Miguel expresses his cultural and personal pride in being barefoot and the toughness of his feet. The outreach counselor is wise to listen. The worker thereby comes to a new understanding of Miguel's world and what he values. In turn, this enabled the worker to reframe his offer in a culturally sensitive manner that respected Miguel's preference for sandals and his choice of when to wear them. Miguel is therefore empowered to accept the offer, rather than potentially feeling that we are not listening to his wants/needs, or perhaps disrespected or shamed over being barefoot and impoverished. This also honors mutuality and autonomy, rather than the outreach counselor playing the role of expert and authority.

If our hope is to do person-centered work, then observing, listening, and attempting to understand a person's words, ideas, and values is a good place to start. Some of this was accomplished by listening to Miguel's story and tuning into his telling of childhood experiences in Puerto Rico. This is facilitated by both understanding and finding mutually acceptable words that furthers a welcomed and trusting communication. I call this building the playground of language. It is important to note that over time, clients provide us with critical feedback as to what words and ideas are welcomed on the playground of language. In this case, Miguel welcomes the idea and goal of finding affordable housing, but clearly expresses his distaste for the word "elder." In his world, the term "elder" denotes being feeble, weak and rejected by others. So, the onus is now on the outreach counselor to find a mutually acceptable term that will help promote Miguel's goal of finding affordable housing.

Excerpt from Miguel's narrative (Levy, 2018) – Part 2

The question was whether or not there was a way to develop a common language with Miguel that would empower him to accept housing for elders. In response to Miguel's negative reaction, I joined with him by sharing my dislike for the term "elder," stating, "People often believe that I am older than my actual age, but I let them know that what's important is my state of mind. I am young at heart and I believe that you are too!" Miguel smiled and nodded in agreement. I continued, "Besides, with age comes wisdom, so perhaps we should consider folks who are over sixty to be wise men. People who have been here the longest often know the most." In this manner, I reframed the notion of being an elder to a more positive reference that Miguel could more actively consider and hopefully accept.

He then went on to share with me the wisdom of his grandmother and the hard lessons his father taught him, while growing up in Puerto Rico. By the end of our session, we were able to laugh together about the need to rename elder housing as "Homes for the Wise" or simply "60 and Over Housing." We entered the next phase of Common Language development by agreeing to some useful and acceptable terminology. In a manner of speaking, we were creating a playground of language from which we could further explore current linguistic connections and future possibilities to guide our work.

The next time Miguel and I met, we discussed his hard road to homelessness and how he deserved a better life, which included having a home. I then drew from our playground of language and brought up the prospects of applying for "60 and Over Housing," so he could have an affordable place to live. In this manner, I was speaking or *utilizing* common words and phrases that we both agreed were a better descriptor of elder housing. Miguel seemed interested, but still a bit hesitant around being labeled as an "elder." I assured him that we could show up at the housing authority together and inform them of our preference for the term "60 and Over Housing." While they may not be willing to change the words on the housing application, we could both voice and write our opinion down for them and others to see.

This plan resonated well with Miguel, and so we contracted for services. Our next task was to fill out the subsidized housing application for seniors. Miguel signed a release of information and I further bridged him over to the worker (aka: Housing Specialist) at the Housing Authority by calling her in advance in preparation for our arrival. This consisted of some advocacy, while also giving the housing authority worker some advance warning of the particularities of Miguel's situation, and his sensitivity to the term "elder."

My engagement process with the Housing Specialist went well. She understood Miguel's situation and promised to be sensitive. She allowed us to write suggestions for terms that would be synonymous with elder housing, but also made it clear that she would not and could not change the actual terminology on the application. This was enough of an accommodation to empower Miguel to effectively take part in the application process for subsidized housing. Ultimately, I was able to form a common language with Miguel that bridged him to the language of the system, while remaining true to our agreed-upon ideas, words and values.

In this manner, Miguel was successfully transitioned over to a new house of language of the Housing authority and eventually received acceptance into subsidized housing for people of 60 years and over. We had successfully completed the last phase of Common Language Construction (see Table 4, p. 45) by bridging together two different interpretations of housing for seniors. Approximately three months after completing the application, he moved into his new place, and welcomed me into his home for weekly outreach counseling visits.

Once Miguel was successfully housed, our work continued to help assure housing stabilization. Major aims of outreach counseling consist of helping people transition to housing and cultivating pathways to treatment. A primary concern that Miguel had was feeling isolated from others, so, much of our post-housing work focused on building community connections. This included the challenge of referring him to a local Senior Center, which brought up similar concerns as our initial work in regard to subsidized housing. The term "senior" was a bit less charged than "elder," and so it was easier to reframe as a term that denotes respect for people who have more life experience. Together, we would laugh and say "No juniors allowed at the Senior Center!" My use of humor and Miguel's willingness to join in showed evidence that we were on the same wavelength, or working from the same playground of language. Fortunately, Miguel agreed to a tour of the center and immediately felt a sense of belonging when he met a staff member who was also from Puerto Rico, and fluent in Spanish.

Table 4: Stages of Common Language Development[6]

Stages	Goals & Interventions
Understand Language	Attempt to understand a homeless person's world by learning the meaning of his or her gestures, words, values and actions. Interventions include observing, listening, reflection, and directly asking what particular words and phrases mean, as well as learning and exploring further what is important to the client.
Utilize Language	Promote understanding by developing and using a mutually agreeable set of terms. Build, modify, and use gestures, words, and phrases from the playground of common language based on the client's cues. Interventions include utilizing common language to ask client questions, explore the outreach worker's role, verbalize client's aspirations, and jointly define goals.
Bridge Language	Connect and integrate the common language developed between client and worker with other systems of language as defined by available services and resources (i.e., housing authorities, Social Security, medical services, mental health clinic, self-help groups, vocational programs, etc.). Interventions include connecting resources and services directly to client's goals, reframing commonly used words and phrases by targeted resources and services to be consistent with the playground of language developed by worker and client. Preparing for interviews via role play and accompanying the client may also be helpful. Prepare intake personnel of needed resources and services for the language that the client speaks. If certain phrases or terms may trigger a negative reaction, reframe and redefine these terms whenever possible, or seek accommodation.

Originally published: Levy, J. S. (2013). Pretreatment Guide for Homeless Outreach & Housing First: Helping Couples, Youth, and Unaccompanied Adults

---

[6] The process of Common Language Construction is based on ideas and concepts drawn from phenomenology and Narrative Psychology. Heidegger's book *On the Way to Language* (1971), as well as Epston & White's selected papers (1989-1991), among others, influenced the formation of Table 4.

Questions for Consideration

Q1: How did the outreach counselor construct a common language with Miguel?

_____

_____

_____

_____

Here's a helpful hint: Review the text for particular words or phrases that promoted a positive communication by resonating with his values.

Q2: How did the worker "Bridge Language" (See Table 4 above) between Miguel and housing resources?

_____

_____

_____

_____

Here's a helpful hint: Think about specific strategies that supported the transition to a needed housing resource.

Q3: If you were the outreach worker, what would you do differently or in addition?

_____

_____

_____

_____

_____

_____

Here's a helpful hint: Reflect upon your own work and the types of assessments and strategies that may help guide the outreach worker's interventions with Miguel.

Reflections and Possibilities

The goal of outreach is to be welcomed into our prospective client's house of language and to develop pathways to the houses of language that define essential resources/services such as Social Security Benefits, AA/NA Groups, and Mental Health Clinics, Subsidized Housing resources, and many others. This requires the willingness of the worker to tune in to what is actually being said, as well as the client's unsaid (contextual and personal meaning), experimenting with language utilization, or perhaps a bit of playfulness with words as we attempt to establish connections between others and needed resources. Bakhtin states (1981, p. 342), "Language, for the individual consciousness, lies on the borderline between oneself and the other. The word in language is half someone else's." In essence, we own only half of a word. Its meaning is ultimately shared between the sender and the receiver. This is consistent with Derrida's post-modern philosophy of language (1976) that views our communication as a relational, creative and playful process in which the meanings of words are subject to change, yet contextually defined.

This is why the first and most critical step of Common Language Construction (see Table 4, p. 45) begins with listening and then questioning to better *understand* a person's words, ideas, and values, along with the goal of *utilizing* a common language to enhance communication, followed by *bridging* language to needed resources and services.

Here, Miguel and the outreach counselor develop a playground of language to further their communication and person-centered work. Miguel clearly objects to the term "elder," so the worker needs to reframe this word and Miguel's perceived negative connotations.

The outreach counselor accomplishes this by using a neutral or uncharged descriptor of Miguel being over sixty years of age and therefore can be prioritized for affordable housing. An additional Pretreatment strategy was to work with Miguel to explore the positive connotations of the word "senior." This was carefully done by the counselor using Miguel's respect for his grandmother's wisdom, which provided a meaningful personal pathway to rename and reframe (bridging language) "elder housing" as "homes for the wise." The worker then further solidified this connection by humorously stating, "No juniors allowed at the senior center!" At that moment the worker and the client formed a "being here" connection (understanding both the said and unsaid), as evidence by them laughing together at the word play they had jointly developed.

These accomplishments (understanding, utilizing, and bridging language) were used to solidify referrals to both "Elder" Housing subsidies and the "Senior" Center for community support services. The outreach counselor mirrored a similar process of common language construction with the staff from both places to help them better understand Miguel's world and how this was reflected through his nuanced use of language. The staff was empowered by bridging their language to Miguel's, and thereby supported him through the process of transition and adaptation to their services and resources. This resulted in Miguel getting an affordable apartment, and becoming a member of the Senior Center, but not without multiple future challenges of maintaining these gains. If interested in a greater detail and more nuanced approach to outreach counseling, you can read Miguel's full narrative in the book, *Cross-Cultural Dialogues on Homelessness* (Levy with Johnson, 2018).

The aim of this example was to illustrate better understanding, utilizing, and bridging particular words and ideas within the personal and cultural context of the client. Next, we now move to working with more complex phrases, deeply held beliefs and values. Example 3-2 introduces us to Andrew who is far more reticent to engage in outreach services than Miguel.

Example 3-2: Excerpt from Andrew's narrative (Levy, 2004; Levy, 2010)

Andrew is a 48-year-old African-American male who has been homeless without any source of sustainable income for the past 18 years. He has spent several years living outdoors, but over the past eight months, he has been able to maintain himself at a shelter in Boston, MA. The outreach clinician, who visits the shelter, is a 36-year-old white, middle class, male social worker. This clinician has known Andrew for approximately four months. Andrew is cautious and has managed to secure a bed in the corner of the room next to the back wall that provides a good view of the shelter layout. He is often sitting up in his bed mumbling or laughing to himself, while remaining keenly aware of his surroundings. The past meetings between Andrew and the social worker have been brief and have never led to substantial conversation. Nevertheless, Andrew has seen this worker engage others, and has ascertained enough information from past meetings to be aware of the social worker's role at the shelter. Andrew would often angrily reject the outreach clinician's efforts to engage by bluntly stating that he did not want to be bothered in his home. This did not discourage the social worker, because he viewed the engagement process as often long and tenuous when encountering long-term homeless individuals with significant trauma.

The outreach clinician approached Andrew and gave a friendly greeting. Andrew responded with angry affect and said, "Don't you understand? I am no longer playing the game!" The social worker replied, "I respect you wanting or needing some space... What do you mean by game?" In turn, Andrew stated, "Look... I've been toyed with before and it's not right! I want you to know... I want everyone to know that I am not playing anymore... Listen, yesterday I saw a dollar on the street... Do you think I picked it up? That's what they want me to do, but I am no sucker! I am sitting it out and just watching, while others make fools of themselves!" The social worker calmly responded, "I think I have a sense of what you're saying: you don't want others to take advantage of you... Who could blame you for that?" Andrew, now more animated, quickly answered, "How could you possibly understand? Look, I had a whole career taken from me... I've been mentally murdered!" Andrew paused, and then with some discernible laughter stated, "Do you know what it is like to be mentally murdered?" The social worker replied, "You're right, no one could fully understand that unless they go through it themselves. I must admit that I don't know what it means to be mentally murdered... Could you tell me?" Andrew calmly responded, while walking away, "I've said enough for now... Besides, I am in the midst of my own research."

Questions for Consideration

Q1: What cultural divides must the Outreach counselor navigate in order to successfully engage with Andrew?

_____

_____

_____

_____

_____

Here's a helpful hint: Think broadly about the term "cultural divide" as identifying an array of differences between two people. Additionally, think about how this differs from the cultural divides in Miguel's story.

Q2: What does Andrew value?

_____

_____

_____

_____

Here's a helpful hint: Think about his strengths and expressed interests.

Q3: If you were the outreach worker, what words or ideas would you want to explore further?

_____

_____

_____

_____

Here's a helpful hint: Focus in on Andrew's challenges, as well as his values, needs and wants.

Q4: During your next round of outreach, how would you engage Andrew in further conversation?

_____

_____

_____

Here's a helpful hint: Begin where Andrew is least angry and therefore perhaps more accepting. Brainstorm two questions that you could use (consult table 4 – Stages of Common Language Development p. 45).

Reflections and Possibilities

Andrew is an African American male in his late 40s. He has experienced long term homelessness, poverty, racism, and associated trauma. In addition, he may have significant mental health concerns. In contrast, the outreach clinician is a white male, mid-30s, currently living in an apartment and socio-economically identified as low middle-class. There are often multiple cultural divides that need to be crossed in order to attain successful engagement, most notably race, culture, and socio-economic status.

Andrew utilizes some colorful language and the worker could benefit from learning more about his said and unsaid meanings. These terms include "not playing the game" and "mental murder." Here, the worker directly asks Andrew what he means by mental murder, though he only receives a partial answer. It does appear to correspond with the loss of his career, status, and becoming homeless. Emotionally, Andrew shares much of this in an angry tone, so it is important for the worker to understand that there are legitimate causes for anger such as mistreatment from others, poverty, racism, and homelessness. Therefore, it is essential for the counselor to learn how to withstand, as well as appreciate expressions of anger, while promoting a safe and open dialogue.

Andrew appears to value his safety and dignity as evidenced by his surveying the shelter layout for potential threats, and his sharing of apparent trauma (mental murder and loss of vocation and/or career status), as well as him refusing to pick up a dollar from the street. Finally, Andrew shares his research interests. In Narrative Psychology circles (Epston & White, 1992; Freedman & Combs, 1996) this can be viewed as a "sparkling moment" and perhaps an opportunity to "work with the exception" to the other problems that were angrily stated. Following this line of thinking, the outreach counselor would be wise to inquire more about Andrew's research as a means of engagement, as this may be an area for a more respectful and dignified dialogue, rather than a white, male, professional trying to engage an impoverished black male in regard to being homeless and in need. Other possibilities for further engagement include a focus on safety, as Andrew appears to value that as well.

Excerpt from Andrew's Narrative (Levy, 2004; Levy, 2010) – Part 2

The outreach clinician once again approached Andrew and said, "So how's your research going?" Andrew replied with a slightly raised voice, "You wouldn't believe it if I told you. Do you think I am just doing nothing and wasting my time? I like to read books, study... Do you think I want to be with these people? My body might be here, but my mind is somewhere else!" The worker responded, "You are obviously well educated. I've noticed that you don't talk much to others and you appear to keep your focus... Most people would be distracted in this environment." Andrew then said, "You're right about that! If you see me talking it's probably to myself. I don't care if people think I am crazy... I am too busy computing numbers and studying time travel." The clinician quickly and enthusiastically stated, "Wow... Time travel!" Andrew smiled and said, "You know, Einstein got it wrong... It's possible because it's not about moving bodies through space!" The worker responded, "Hmm... This is quite interesting... What is it about?" Andrew once again smiled and calmly stated, "It's about my research and I can't divulge much except to say that our minds can travel without our bodies." The clinician then smiled and said, "yes... I could envision our thoughts traveling!" Andrew winked and said, "You got the general idea, but I am not going to share any details of my research." The clinician responded, "I can respect that you're doing important work and that you want to keep it private." Andrew smiled to himself, without any eye contact toward the worker, and then abruptly walked away.

The worker approached Andrew approximately one week later and said, "Hi Andrew! Are you still contemplating your research? Andrew responded, "Quite naturally... It takes time and discipline." The outreach clinician then stated, "I understand... Would it help to have your own place so you can study without distraction?" Andrew then said with a slightly raised voice, "I told you... I am not playing that game... You have no idea what I've been through!" The worker quickly responded, "It sounds like you've been hurt." Andrew then responded with angry affect, "That doesn't begin to describe it... I've been completely stressed out... mentally murdered! I've had my career taken away! Look... I've been through too much! Even if I could get a place to do my research, I have no money to pay for it." The clinician then said, "I believe you when you tell me that you've been through too much... If you'd like, we could go to the nurse's station, which is private, and you could help me understand what you've been through. The stressful situations you've been through sounds awful. After all, you said your career was taken away... Let's talk about that." Andrew then agreed to talk in private.

Questions for Consideration

Q1: How did the worker re-engage and what words or ideas appear to resonate well with Andrew? Why?

_____

_____

_____

_____

_____

Here's a helpful hint: Think about how the worker tried to appeal to Andrew's strengths.

Q2: How have the meaning of the terms "Not Playing the Game" and "Mental Murder" begun to evolve within the context of their conversation? What do you suppose is Andrew's said/unsaid meaning of these terms?

_____

_____

_____

_____

Here's a helpful hint: Review the context of Andrew's word usage and think about what he is trying to communicate to the worker.

Q3: How does the counselor begin to utilize Andrew's terms (language) to promote the work?

_____

_____

_____

_____

Here's a helpful hint: Look for the different ways that the worker reflects some of the same words and terms that Andrew uses and think about ways of doing this more.

Reflections and Possibilities

The worker's strategy of reengagement wisely begins with an appreciative inquiry of how Andrew's research is going. This opens up a new area for potential dialogue that is not problem focused and also upholds Andrew's dignity by respecting his expertise, rather than the counselor playing the role of expert. Andrew is initially receptive to this and shares that his research is on time travel. Rather than ignoring, questioning or doubting the veracity of Andrew's research, the counselor enthusiastically embraces the idea. The counselor then advances their dialogue by offering the goal of attaining an office space to support Andrew's research, which could also be seen as a first step on working toward a housing placement.

Although Andrew initially rejects this idea, the worker successfully echoes Andrew's concerns (utilizing Andrews words and ideas) that he has been through all too much, many stressful situations, and has had his career taken away. This is done in tandem with making an offer to speak privately in a manner that now has greater resonance in Andrew's world. Andrew agrees to the offer to privately share more of his story, including mistreatment by others. The outreach counselor's hope is to gain a better understanding of Andrew's narrative and thereby explore possible pretreatment pathways to housing and recovery.

Upon entering the nurse's office, Andrew shares his story of oppression from white society, being forced out of his residence due to a fire and losing his job as a Transit Authority employee through no fault of his own. His painful journey into homelessness and being stuck there for eighteen long years is communicated through the term "Mental Murder." The Outreach counselor is able to fulfill his role as interpreter and bridge builder by utilizing the terms "trauma" and "loss," which Andrew welcomes onto their playground of language. Andrew endorses this idea by stating, "Yes… that's what I call 'Mental Murder'… only my body and soul survived the war."

The link between "trauma" and "mental murder" (bridging language) made through empathic, careful listening and word play is crucial to the success of their work. The counselor is able to bridge from Andrew's house of language which now includes mental health terms such as trauma, loss, and stress to Social Security's house of language that's centered on "disability" impeding one's ability to work. The case is successfully made to Andrew that he is deserving of benefits due to the trauma and its debilitating effects. Eventually, Andrew gave the worker permission by to work on attaining social security benefits as a means to pay for an apartment with an office space to continue his research. Their ongoing work and the resulting success of attaining benefits, housing placement, and initial engagement into recovery-based community services is highly nuanced. A more detailed and complete review can be found in Chapter 6 of *Homeless Narratives & Pretreatment Pathways* (Levy, 2010).

This example demonstrates that constructing a common language is a powerful tool. It can dissolve cultural divides, while also empowering the worker and client to join in a meaningful search to achieve mutually defined goals. Understanding and utilizing a common language helps us to really listen, improve our communication, and clarify whether or not our words and actions are resonating well with the client. The last phase of "bridging language" is critical to supporting client transitions to needed resources and services. The next chapter on ecological considerations more thoroughly explores the process of transition and adaptation to new ideas, people, and environments.

References

Bakhtin, M. M. ([1935] 1981). *'Discourse in the novel,' in The Dialogic Imagination: Four essays by M. M. Bakhtin, ed M. Holquist, trans. C. Emerson and M. Holquist.* Austin, Texas: University of Texas Press.

Berger, P. & Luckman, T. (1966). *The social construction of reality.* New York: Doubleday.

Boring, E. G. (1930). "A New Ambiguous Figure." *Amer. J. Psychology* **42**, 444. Derrida, J. (1976). *Of Grammatology*, trans. G. C. Spivak. Batimore: The John Hopkins University Press.

Epston, D. & White, M. (1992). *Experience, contradiction, narrative, and imagination: Selected papers of David Epston and Michael White, 1989-1991.* Adelaide, Australia: Dulwich Centre Publications.

Freedman, J. & Combs, G. (1996). *Narrative therapy: The social construction of preferred realities.* New York: W. W. Norton Company, Inc.

Heidegger, M., (1971). *On the way to language. trans. Hertz, P.* New York: Harper & Row.

Hill, W. E. (1915, November). "My Wife and My Mother-in-Law." *Puck* **16**, 11.

Levy, J. S. (2004). Pathway to a Common Language: A Homeless Outreach Perspective. Families in Society: *The Journal of Contemporary Human Services*, 85(3), 371-378.

Levy, J. S. (2010). *Homeless narratives & pretreatment pathways: From words to housing.* Ann Arbor, MI: Loving Healing Press.

Levy, J. S. (2013). *Pretreatment guide for homeless outreach & housing first: Helping couples, youth, and unaccompanied adults.* Ann Arbor, MI: Loving Healing Press.

Levy, J. S. with Johnson, R. (2018). *Cross-cultural dialogues on homelessness: From pretreatment strategies to psychological environments.* Ann Arbor, MI: Loving Healing Press.

Perls, F. S. (1969). *Gestalt Therapy Verbatim.* Moab, Utah: Real People Press.

4 Ecological Considerations: Supporting Transitions

Introduction

The third principle of a Pretreatment approach is Ecological Considerations. It is based on a "Person in Environment" perspective (Germain & Gitterman, 1980) or examining how a person has attained equilibrium or is at disequilibrium within their given environment. In particular, our focus is on the worker's and client's processes of transition and adaptation to new people, ideas, services and resources, or any particular environment or system they work or reside in. This is a universal principle in that we all go through processes of transition and adaptation to new environments in an attempt to establish an acceptable equilibrium or balance. The central question is: how can we best support these natural processes?

This is true for transition and adaptation challenges one may face in regard to harsh living environments such as the streets or a bus station, or in regard to orienting to an outreach counselor, treatment based services, or a new apartment and/or neighborhood, etc. By tuning into these natural processes, outreach counselors are in a position to observe strengths and challenges by understanding what works vs. what doesn't work through past and present attempts at transitions. To apply this principle is to reflect on these processes with clients in order to bring forth conscious awareness of particular transitions at hand and then plan successful strategies.

Psychologically Informed Environments (PIE) is another ecological approach that promotes the fit of person in environment. PIE was introduced to the UK's homelessness services network by Helen Keats, Robin Johnson and others (2012). It is trauma-informed, and effectively engages and better serves homeless persons who were diagnosed with personality disorders (people with complex trauma and multiple needs). It has also been used to design small transitional settings (homeless hostels), physical and social environments, to provide more welcoming person-centered environments that are psychologically informed to the particular homeless subgroup it serves. If you are interested in learning more about this approach, it is discussed at length in a book I jointly edited with Robin Johnson, entitled *Cross-Cultural Dialogues on Homelessness: From Pretreatment Strategies to Psychologically Informed Environments* (Levy with Johnson, 2018).

Exercise 4-1: Brainstorm: Strategies to Support Transitions

Identify different strategies or approaches that help people through the process of transition and adaptation to new environments.

_____

_____

_____

_____

Here's a helpful hint: Take a moment to reflect on the different ways you support your clients through the referral process to new environments, people, resources and services... Challenge yourself to see how many you can name.

Discussion

The process of transition and adaptation is happening all around us. As outreach counselors, street medicine practitioners, case managers, Housing First or Permanent Supportive Housing staff, it is our job to tune in to this reality. I call this "catching the transition bus." This is an opportunity to enhance engagement and thereby set the stage for further work. When looking through the ecological lens, we are sensitive to observing any signs of distress, or "person in environment" disequilibrium, and are ready to respond by offering assistance in supporting critical transitions. For example, if a shelter case manager or outreach counselor observes someone entering shelter for the first time, it provides the opportunity to offer a tour or orientation to transition the person to their new surroundings, while simultaneously promoting the engagement process.

Ecological considerations inform both our on-the-ground assessments and interventions with clients, as well as integrating our programs with new funding opportunities. The outreach teams I manage recently received new monies to utilize short-term motel stays (three to five days) in tandem with our daily outreach services. We decided to utilize these motel stays to broadly support transitions; whether it be to new housing opportunities, attending interviews for employment, safe landing for institutional discharges, or to enhance the engagement process with an outreach worker by supporting transition to the next engagement phase of contracting. Further, this facilitated our work by allowing us to easily locate and then meet with someone in a safe space for completing applications for housing, employment, benefits, etc. We also provide safe temporary motel placement when a safe shelter is unavailable for those who refuse to access shelter, yet are at risk due to harsh environmental change via extreme weather conditions (i.e., freezing-cold weather, major snow storms, floods, heat waves).

We must recognize that the very first transition we support is to our own presence. It often begins with desensitization as an integral part of the early engagement process. There are effective strategies that passively reinforce the engagement process, while defining our role. This is done by doing outreach in the proximity of the client with others (gradual exposure), or approaching the person with need items in hand as an initial offering (reinforcement), while respecting a personal space (signaling safety). We may continue this desensitization process to our specific role as an outreach counselor through our initial communications that center on the person's needs/wants, and listening to their use of language, so that we can frame out our offering in a way that resonates with the client (upholding person's autonomy/sense of control). This supports the transition to the offering or even to a new idea that can be considered and reflected upon (contemplated) further by the prospective client. Finally, "Bridging Language," as discussed in the previous chapter, is our way of introducing and exploring potential resources and services for the client to contemplate as a match to their needs/wants and may lead to generating an initial mutually acceptable goal or contract for services.

Once a person-centered relationship that is guided by mutually acceptable goals is established, the question becomes how to support transitions to new environments including safe housing or shelter placement, support services, treatment and other resources/services. Basic orientation, preparation, education, skill building, understanding barriers and problem solving in regard to establishing these new connections are an essential part of our work. This includes supporting transition and adaption by accompanying people to key appointments, strengthening coping skills, utilizing role play to prepare, and helping the client to gain perspective through education about new settings, and exploration about what has worked vs. what hasn't worked in the past.

Exercise 4-2: Psychosocial Rehabilitation Strategies

Describe a time when you helped a client by developing skills, adding supports, and/or making environmental modifications to support the transition and adaptation process.

_____

_____

_____

_____

_____

Here's a helpful hint: This may include restoring their equilibrium with the current environment, or supporting transitions to new environments.

Discussion

Our work can benefit greatly by the application of Psychosocial Rehabilitation strategies (Anthony, et al., 1990). A Psychosocial Rehabilitation approach is person-centered, strengths-based, and begins with a focus on people's goals. A counselor can address barriers to achieving one's goals by enhancing supports or building a responsive support network, and skill development such as strengthening ways of coping, as well as considering environmental modifications to improve the fit of person in environment.

A critical, yet often overlooked, element of Psychosocial Rehabilitation is to consider environmental modifications as a reasonable accommodation to promote greater access, transition and adaptation. For example, a person with mobility challenges who utilizes a wheelchair may require an apartment with wheelchair accessible ramps and modifications to widen entrance and exit ways. Similarly, when working with someone with a history of not being able to cook safely, we have exchanged stoves and ovens for microwaves, as well as located folks near meal programs to promote easy access for prepared food. Certain mental health concerns can also be addressed through an enhanced support network, developing skills, and environmental modifications. Over the years, we have worked with some clients who periodically yell or scream to express their distress and thereby inadvertently disturb neighbors. In response, we have implemented environmental modifications to help absorb sound (e.g., introducing thick rugs, tapestry on the walls, and upholstered furniture), worked on improving coping skills to reduce stress and outbursts, as well as added additional check-ins with an outreach counselor and safety planning (access to 24/7 crisis hotline) to provide increased support. This enabled many of our clients to achieve greater stability, and thereby experience a sense of success by staying in housing, rather than compounding their trauma through additional failures.

The following examples, questions and reflections will help us to better envision some of the many ways to support folks through the process of transition and adaptation to new environments.

Example 4-1: Excerpt from Judy's Narrative (Levy, 2018)

When I first met Judy, a white female in her early 60s, I was immediately struck by her weathered appearance, strength, and candor. She is among the long-term homeless who frequent several small towns in Western MA. Sadly, Judy experienced early life difficulties, ending up in foster care due to extensive abuse/neglect by her biological parents. During her teen years, she dropped out of high school, contended with alcohol/drug abuse, and was briefly incarcerated for public intoxication and disturbing the peace with loud diatribes about the ills of capitalist society. Since early adulthood, she has spent more than twenty years surviving the outside elements, temporarily staying in shelters, and occasionally ending up in jail for assault and/or theft.

Judy suffers from schizophrenia, which is her principal diagnosis. She also has a history of intermittent alcohol abuse and significant trauma. During the past two years, Judy's functioning has steadily declined as reflected by more frequent verbally aggressive interactions with fellow community members. Unfortunately, this has led to run-ins with the police and an increased number of arrests, as well as an uptick in short-term involuntary psychiatric inpatient stays.

Many times in the past, we have offered Judy both housing and treatment options, which she adamantly refused. Like so many others, Judy does not believe that she has mental illness or substance abuse issues, and so she takes particular offense to anyone who insinuates or even hints at this being a concern.

Pretreatment Strategies

Here, we join Judy and the outreach counselor, from the PATH team I manage, in an attempt to support her transition from living outside to accessing the local shelter and affordable housing opportunities. The counselor interacted with Judy at least twice a week.

Over time, Judy responded in a positive manner to the consistent non-demanding presence of the outreach worker and his offering of basic need items such as socks, water, and an occasional five-dollar gift card to the local donut shop. It also helped that the outreach counselor was able to speak Judy's language in a way that upheld her values of a non-materialistic philosophy, thereby meeting the client where she was at. This was an effective strategy as evidenced by Judy referring to others in a judgmental and condescending tone as "the dummies with the money" before turning to the outreach worker and saying, "but you're all right." The worker's past history of homelessness played an important role in his ability to successfully connect with Judy in a compassionate manner.

She now trusted him and engaged more readily, though she hadn't yet agreed to work on specific goals. Through our clinical supervision discussions, the counselor and I focused on how to frame an "offer" for Judy in a way that might resonate in her world. During our case narrative exploration, the outreach counselor shared that Judy had complained on several occasions about her belongings getting stolen, as well as a concern about various rodents — chipmunks and squirrels — rummaging through her bags. We both understood that Judy valued keeping her personal property safe, and so we decided to address these immediate concerns as a potential point of further engagement and contracting for services.

The outreach counselor was advised to offer housing as a means of protecting Judy's bags from the elements, rodents, and others. Judy liked this idea, so keeping her and her stuff safe became our primary focus. However, there were some significant challenges due to her untreated psychiatric issues and baseline behaviors that consisted of loud protests about her homeless plight, while directing blame and anger at anyone in the immediate vicinity. Unfortunately, this also included potential neighbors and landlords.

As the winter months approached, we began working with the local shelter and housing provider to consider accommodating Judy. We explained to Judy that if she could stay at the shelter during the coldest nights of winter and thereby stay safe, we would also advocate with the local shelter and housing provider to prioritize her for affordable housing. The outreach counselor joined with Judy through a common language by referring to her strongly held value of safety (from others and freezing temperatures) and the option of affordable housing to keep her belongings secure and free from pest-damage.

Since we attend weekly homelessness services meetings, the outreach counselor, shelter staff, and I took the opportunity to jointly develop a plan on how to respond to Judy's disruptive behaviors, while allowing her to have shelter access throughout the winter months. This also meant addressing the shelter's policy that once a person enters the shelter, they need to stay the entire night. If Judy left in the middle of the night, she would be denied reentry, which in the past occurred on multiple occasions. In essence, we developed a plan of reasonable accommodation to provide Judy with a renewed and more realistic opportunity to successfully leave the streets during the height of winter to the relative security of our small, local homeless shelter. "Reasonable accommodation" is a legal right in the United States for people with disabilities, which can be utilized when their particular issues related to disability interfere with access to needed services and/or resources. In this case, Judy had been denied access due to her inability to follow the shelter policy of residing inside for the entire night without leaving. This was in part due to Judy's history of trauma, which was at times triggered by staying in close quarters with others, so her need to leave directly connected to her "disability" and/or mental instability.

In response, we offered the shelter supervisor and Judy an anger management Pretreatment strategy that allowed her to leave the premises whenever she felt over-stimulated or overwhelmed, knowing that she was welcome to return upon calming herself down. The outreach clinician reviewed this plan with Judy and worked with her on strengthening coping strategies. This allowed Judy to successfully utilize the shelter on a more frequent basis than in the past. We were therefore able to prioritize her for affordable housing.

Questions for Consideration

Q1: What does Judy value?

_____

_____

_____

_____

_____

Here's a helpful hint: Consider Judy's "said and unsaid" values based on both her words and actions.

Q2: How does the worker incorporate Judy's values with transition planning?

_____

_____

_____

_____

_____

Here's a helpful hint: Consider how the specific transition plan for accessing shelter and housing connects to Judy's adaptations, concerns, and daily struggles.

Reflections and Possibilities

Judy had experienced multiple episodes of homelessness, trauma and loss throughout her life. This resulted in some entrenched adaptive behaviors to living in harsh environments without the advantages of a responsive support network of friends and allies. As a result, she has learned how to independently survive on the streets, while rejecting help from others whom she'd perceived as threatening to her sense of safety, autonomy, and privacy.

Or, we can surmise that she values her safety, autonomy, independence, and privacy, as well as things that will promote her sense of survival and wellbeing. The counselor's understanding of Judy's values and interests is an important step toward getting where she is at.

Through the aid of supervision (co-vision) and reflective practice, the outreach counselor is empowered to construct an offering via a common language that can resonate in Judy's world. The outreach counselor connects with Judy's direct concerns of keeping her belongings safe from others and surviving the impending winter season with plummeting temperatures. This results in the offering of temporary shelter and a housing plan that can be heard and contemplated by Judy because it touches upon her immediate concerns.

The successful articulation and agreement to work on the goals to get inside from the winter elements and to secure housing as a safe place to store her belongings is the framing of the transition process between the worker, Judy, and local shelter staff. The outreach worker needs to be nimble in understanding both the "rules of engagement" (multiple houses of language) with Judy and with potential service and resource providers. In essence, this is engaging both in a common language toward attaining these goals, or "bridging language" between our clients and the resources/services that they need.

The next step, in coordination with the supervisor during co-vision meetings, is to consider specific strategies to support transition to the local shelter, as well as completing the application and prioritization for housing placement. This process is informed by both the client's and provider's past experiences of what has worked vs. what has not worked. For Judy, this included feeling confined, over-stimulated, and at times feeling threatened by others at the shelter. For the provider, this included concerns in regard to managing Judy's outbursts and her breaking of rules by abruptly leaving the shelter as a fight/flight response to feeling threatened and/or mistreated by others.

In response, the outreach counselor engaged both the client and shelter provider staff to develop a mutually acceptable plan. This included advocacy for "reasonable accommodation," thereby highlighting Judy's rights to be safe from the cold and have access affordable housing, as well as helping her to take steps to reduce the frequency of her angry outbursts. With Judy's agreement, a cognitive-behavioral plan allowed her to briefly leave the shelter whenever she felt unsafe, while also committing her to the work of enhancing and practicing her coping skills with the outreach counselor. This resulted in her being able to return back to the shelter without the incident of an angry outburst directed toward shelter staff or other guests. This reasonable accommodation plan gave Judy the opportunity to secure a safe shelter bed with the prioritization for future housing placement. In essence, the sharing of a psycho-logical approach with shelter staff helped Judy manage stress and trauma associated with the shelter environment. The adaptation of the rules of the social environment allowed Judy to become an empowered shelter community member, as opposed to someone who was constantly in violation of the rules.It provided a better fit or Psychologically Informed Environment (PIE) to better meet Judy's needs.

While Judy was not 100% successful at returning to the shelter with her anger in check, her efforts matched with reasonable accommodation allowances by staff were enough. She showed significant improvement, which allowed her to utilize the shelter for the entire winter season. Our success at helping Judy to transition for a short-term stay at a homeless shelter not only opened the door to eventual affordable housing placement, but also taught us a valuable lesson in regard to what future transitional strategies may be helpful. We now turn to Ecological Considerations/Supporting Transitions with a couple via the next example.

Example 4-2: Excerpt from Janice and Michael's Narrative (Levy, 2013)

Janice (W, F, 50s) and Michael (W, M, 50s) have lived together for a long time, mostly camping out-doors as survivalists, as almost all shelters segregate by gender with no accommodation for couples to remain together. Janice presents with multiple and complex needs due to significant and layered trauma. This is reflected in her co-dependent behaviors in response to Michael's alcohol addiction, as well as her depressed mood, labile affect, and bouts of severe anxiety compounded by living in harsh outside environments. Michael comes across as quiet and at times very angry. However, they show no evidence of physical abuse toward one another and have slowly come to trust the outreach counselor. They are a couple who have lived outdoors for the past three years and have finally achieved enough income to consider a temporary stay at a motel.

Here, we join Janice and Michael in their quest to get off the streets and find safe housing. However, it was a journey full of multiple crisis points before they jointly agreed to accept the outreach counselor's help toward this goal. The relationship between crisis and opportunity will be more fully explored in the next chapter, and a full accounting of their narrative is available in chapter 4 of *Pretreatment Guide for Homeless Outreach & Housing First* (2013).

Supporting Transitions: Easier Said than Done

By the New Year I was able to make arrangements for Janice and Mike to move into a cheap motel with a monthly rate tailored to cost them most of their combined welfare checks. This came to $500 per month and left them with only $106 per month spending money and about $45 in food stamps. However, when one factored in Mike's propensity to drink and Janice's inclination to raise additional money by collecting and returning refundable cans, their lack of funds was not necessarily a concern. They also continued to attend a daily community meal, which provided them with free food, some daily structure, and much needed socialization. In exchange for our hard work to establish a new residence, they both promised to attend healthcare appointments and to work with me on a budgeting plan to assure payment of rent. The motel manager agreed to rent them a place because I was able to get a security deposit via the Salvation Army, and he valued my support services.

Over the next three months, I visited Janice and Michael twice a week at their motel room. Fortunately, I was successful in helping them to qualify for Social Security benefits. Their combined income was now greater than $1000 per month. We also made inroads with Janice establishing a therapeutic connection with a counselor via the local mental health clinic. Michael continued to drink and remained at high risk for liver disease. He was told by his daughter that he could meet his granddaughter for the first time, if he could attain sobriety. In response, Michael was able to curtail his drinking intermittently, though not enough to actually visit his granddaughter. This remained some far off ideal that he could strive for, but could never quite reach. On the positive end, Mike would sometimes attend AA meetings and successfully meet with his primary doctor.

In time, their motel room appeared increasingly cluttered, and there was evidence to suggest that Janice had a hoarding issue. It was very important to engage Janice in the process of determining what to donate, store, or trash. This needed to be done in a very sensitive manner because she showed an emotional connection to her growing collection of items and would not tolerate a quick process of simply removing things without careful consideration. This was her stuff and she understandably wanted a sense of control over the threatening process of reducing the clutter. In response, my weekly visits focused on straightening out the hotel room with their active participation. This consisted of us removing trash, as well as trimming down their belongings. Specific interventions were utilized to define the livable space versus setting up shelves and allocated areas for storage items. Once these areas were fully utilized, we jointly packed up some things to be moved to a local storage facility versus throwing away or donating less needed stuff. Michael and Janice now had enough money to pay a fee, so some personal items were sent over to a storage unit until they could get a larger place. This was more of a harm reduction approach to hoarding by removing clutter and reorganizing space in a sensitive manner. Janice's rate of acquisition remained an issue for future intervention, though my efforts were successful in the short term at retaining their tenancy.

Her mental health clinician (therapist) was apprised of this issue, and Janice was encouraged to share her challenges, thoughts, and feelings around removing and limiting future acquisition of items. In addition, I met with Mike and Janice around the first of the month so we could walk over to the bank and make arrangements for their rent to be paid. All in all, this was an effective motel outreach plan based on housing stabilization strategies, but it had a high degree of difficulty to maintain. Consistent visits, remaining sensitive to engagement issues, and hard work kept things going in a positive direction... not perfect, but under control. In this manner, my work had transformed from street outreach to housing support activities though the underlying principles of Pretreatment remained the same. This also provided us with a plan that could be continued, as well as built upon to support their transition to an affordable apartment.

As the last of the winter snow melted and the first crocuses began to bloom, Janice and Michael were offered a subsidized apartment by the local housing authority. They successfully managed the move to a new affordable place. Together we celebrated the fruits of our journey, though we knew full well that things were far from perfect. Michael continued to have episodes of drinking heavily, and his health worsened. Though he remained unreceptive to receiving substance abuse treatment, he frequently expressed his gratitude for having a home. He once said to me, "Through the years I've lost so much, but now I can rest. You just don't know how much I appreciate having a place I can truly call 'home'."

Over the next nine months, we must have visited the emergency room on at least three separate occasions. Eventually, Mike paid the ultimate price. Within one year of being successfully housed, he died at a local hospital with Janice by his side. He was only 52 years old. Janice was heartbroken, but she remained connected with her therapist and together we (Janice, the therapist, and I) managed to pay tribute to Mike and the years that they spent "keeping the bastards at bay." They were survivalists and with Michael's death, Janice was now able to take better care of herself. Of course, this wasn't the happy ending that we had hoped for and strived to achieve. Before his death, Michael found meaning in leaving homelessness behind, and afterward Janice remained housed, while finally getting help for the deep and layered trauma she had experienced throughout her life.

Questions for Consideration

Q1: How does the Outreach Counselor support the transition and adaptation process from living outside to entering a motel room?

_____

_____

_____

_____

_____

_____

Here's a helpful hint: Consider what supported the placement and transition to the motel, as well as what helped to maintain their tenancy there.

Q2: What specific strategies were used to address Janice's hoarding behaviors? Is there anything you would do differently... why or why not?

_____

_____

_____

_____

_____

Here's a helpful hint: Consider how the counselor balances engagement and support, while also addressing tenancy and safety issues that hoarding can cause.

Reflections and Possibilities

The excerpt begins with Michael and Janice already willing to accept placement via a motel. The worker supports their transition in various ways. First is through helping Michael and Janice to attain enough benefits to afford a temporary motel stay. Secondly, advocacy with the Motel manager and a promise to provide ongoing support services were critical to creating the pathway to placement.

After the move into the motel, the worker provided consistent visitation (twice weekly) and worked on various goals toward maintaining tenancy. This included a budgeting plan, availability to provide 1:1 assistance in assuring payment of monthly motel fee, as well as active joint participation in weekly cleaning and decluttering activities. The Pretreatment work completed prior to motel placement resulted in strong person-centered relationships with Janice and Michael. It set the table for the expertise of the outreach counselor to

> Each person's journey of transition and adaptation to new environments is unique, yet it is up to the outreach counselor to find the best ways to support it.

be applied to clinical issues as they arose or became more apparent to both worker and client throughout the transition process.

Once it became evident that Janice had a hoarding issue, an active behavioral-cognitive plan was utilized to promote organization of belongings, clearly demarcate livable space from storage areas, as well as reduce unneeded belongings to more manageable levels. This included engaging both Janice and her therapist to further discuss hoarding issues. We utilized Janice's language to reframe "hoarding" as her need to collect things. The therapist's role was to address how to reduce acquisition of new items, while our work became more focused on removing items from the motel room by either giving them away, or putting them out with the trash, as well as the infrequent transfer of a small number of highly valued items to a storage facility, thereby applying the natural limits of Janice's available space.

The utilization of temporary storage was a harm reduction strategy to balance ongoing engagement with Janice, as power struggles over getting rid of certain items could surely lead to disengagement from services. The small size of the storage unit and the limited shelving and closet space in the motel room would serve as a natural limit they agreed upon, while Janice received ongoing counseling to gain perspective on this issue. Further, in order to protect the hard earned person-centered relationship between the counselor and Janice, the task of reducing items at the motel was *never* the first or last thing discussed. Both the opening and closing conversations by the outreach counselor with Janice and Michael were primarily used to foster continued engagement, as well as reviewing agreed-upon goals to facilitate future work.

In this excerpt, the outreach counselor framed out the advantages of accessing housing as a natural next step to living at a motel and this became possible once Janice and Michael qualified for additional benefits via Social Security and the local housing authority. This was purposely done as a direct response to their playground of language and professed needs, which included their stated goal of getting placed in affordable housing.

However, among the long-term homeless, there are those with such significant trauma and loss that they initially seem unable or perhaps unwilling to accept housing placement. Much of this corresponds to entrenched adaptation strategies to living outside, pride in their ability to survive, and the associated fears, anxiety, and disequilibrium caused by contemplating significant change. For many of these folks, a good first step is a desensitization plan to place their belongings in a safe locale they can access as needed. From there, the outreach counselor may plan to hold some meetings near or at the apartment, bring a need item as a house warming gift, or install a phone at the apartment to assure private communication and the ability to make calls during times of crisis. Another fruitful avenue is for the counselor and client to converse on the advantages of having access to a private bathroom, which inevitably gets a positive response.

Over time this enables the client to gain familiarity and comfort with the apartment without feeling suddenly forced into something that the worker may want to achieve. Timing and pacing matter, and can avoid setbacks. Even upon moving into the apartment, many of our clients may feel too confined. Some manage to adapt by opening windows and maybe even sleeping on the floor, rather than in a bed. Others have a need to take breaks and return to camping out, while continuing to utilize their apartment for bathroom access, showers, phone, and storage. Each person's journey of transition and adaptation to new environments is unique, yet it is up to the outreach counselor to find the best ways to support it.

Transitions to Housing First

During the past fifteen years, I have helped to design and manage several Housing First initiatives including REACH Housing programs (Regional Engagement and Assessment of Chronically Homeless) and various CSPECH services (Community Support for People Experiencing Chronic Homelessness) aimed at providing transition and stabilization services for newly housed, yet highly vulnerable individuals. Housing First Programs with flexible support services have been effective at helping individuals with multiple and complex needs to attain and maintain housing in the community (Bretherton & Pleace, 2015; Stefancic and Tsemberis, 2007; Tsemberis, 2010). These issues include long-term homelessness, severe mental illness, addiction, and major medical issues.

Our approach to supporting people's transitions to housing, as well as taking an initial step toward melting the "pre-contemplation iceberg" to treatment or recovery-based services always begins with a welcoming and orientation to the housing community paired with initial safety planning. This begins with a celebration of arriving at a new residence, which consists of staff (outreach and Housing First staff) providing house warming gifts, needed supplies, and orientation to the local community, as well as a "breaking bread" ceremony of snacks, drink, pastry or cake.

The orientation is completed on the day of the move-in with a review of current supports and phone numbers for any foreseeable crisis or emergency the client is willing to discuss. We always end the first day by highlighting that there are four core responsibilities that any tenant, including ourselves, take on upon moving into housing. This consist of being safe, paying rent, getting along with neighbors, and taking care of property. Finally, the staff makes a joint pledge to the new resident that we are all dedicated to the task of keeping the person housed and safe. The only thing that varies is the number of staff in attendance and the duration of the event based on the tenant's "window of tolerance" and preferences.

A new tenant often ends up struggling with one of the core responsibilities for remaining in good standing with the landlord or their neighbors. When this occurs, we look at this as an opportunity to discuss the need for positive change, so that their tenancy can be preserved. Often this leads to further counsel and contemplation of particular treatment or recovery options to head off an impending housing crisis that may result in eviction. Or sometimes this is the beginning of a decompensation or the development of significant and acute medical and/or mental health issues, or significant increase in addictive behaviors that further interfere with independent functioning and safety of the resident.

All of this presents ample opportunity for further work, as long as we remain engaged in a person-centered relationship based on Pretreatment principles of care. Often, we learn new things together with the resident through each crisis and we are thereby able to modify the initial safety plan. This enables us to respond better to future issues that may arise, culminating in further engagement in harm reduction approaches, recovery or clinical services, as well as a sustained tenancy.

Many times, our transitions to treatment or recovery-based services such as Neighborhood Health Centers, Mental Health Clinics, Recovery Centers, Mental Health Clubhouses, as well as inpatient services via hospitals or detox facilities occur in response to crisis. As many of you already know, there is a natural link between crisis and opportunity for change.

As mentioned earlier, the five principles of Pretreatment are practiced in tandem, so many of the issues discussed are not at all limited to only one principle of care. Further exploration of crisis intervention strategies and supporting transitions to clinical services will be discussed at length in the next chapter.

References

Anthony, W., Cohen, M. & Farkas, M. (1990). *Psychiatric rehabilitation*. Boston University: Center For Psychiatric Rehabilitation.

Bretherton, J. & Pleace, N. (2015). *Housing first in England: An evaluation of nine services*. Center for Housing Policy: University of York.

Germain, C. B. & Gitterman, A. (1980). *The life model of social work process*. New York: Columbia University Press.

Keats, H., Cockersell, P., Johnson, R. & Maguire, N. (2012). *Psychologically informed services; good practice guidance*; London, Dept. Communities and Local Government.

Levy, J. S. (2013). *Pretreatment guide for homeless outreach & housing first: Helping couples, youth, and unaccompanied adults*. Ann Arbor, MI: Loving Healing Press.

Levy, J. S. with Johnson, R. (2018). *Cross-cultural dialogues on homelessness: From* pretreatment strategies to psychological environments. Ann Arbor, MI: Loving Healing Press.

Stefancic, A. & Tsemberis, S. (2007). Housing first for long-term shelter dwellers with psychiatric disabilities in a suburban county: A four-year study of housing access and retention. *The Journal of Primary Prevention*, 28(3-4): 265-279.

Tsemberis, S. (2010). Housing First: Ending homelessness, promoting recovery and reducing cost. In I. Ellen & B. O'Flaherty (eds) *How to House the Homeless*. New York: Russell Sage Foundation

5 Promoting Safety: Harm Reduction and Crisis Intervention

Introduction

The two pillars of the Pretreatment principle of "promoting safety" are Harm Reduction and Crisis Intervention. Our stance in response to *crisis* is more active, directive and assertive than it would be otherwise when addressing safety concerns from a harm reduction philosophy that is meant to minimize risk and increase safety over a period of time.

During times of crisis, we hope to avoid an emergency situation from occurring, so swift action is needed and sometimes these acute situations result in emergency care, inpatient stays, or immediate referrals and placements to essential services and resources (i.e., medical or psychiatric care, detox facilities, shelter beds, respite programs, warming or cooling centers, and other safe spaces) to reduce the likelihood of harm, as well as to provide an immediate opportunity for stability and positive change. My mantra to staff is to "embrace crisis," because therein lays the opportunity for positive change.

Harm Reduction approaches (Marlatt & Tapert, 1993) are focused on providing person-centered support and going at the client's pace, while exploring strategies through a common language to reduce harm and increase safety. These types of interventions are exemplified by an outreach counselor or nurse providing need items such as a clean needle for someone who uses intravenous drugs, or offering a blanket, sleeping bag and/or tent for someone who is sleeping outside and is not inclined to stay at a homeless shelter even under frigid conditions. All of this is done not only to promote safety, but also to establish the working relationship so more work can be accomplished to achieve positive change. As opposed to our direct and active stance during a crisis, our Harm Reduction based assessments and interventions unfold over time and are often more subtle in nature.

Promoting Safety is at the forefront of a Pretreatment approach, as it is assessed and integrated into all of our interventions with folks who present with multiple and complex needs, while residing in harsh and often unsafe environments. Whether it is crisis intervention or utilizing harm reduction strategies, our assessments guide our approach, not our personal inclinations toward passive or active responses. The following exercise and narrative excerpts explore these concepts further with the ever-present goal of promoting safety.

Exercise 5-1: Brainstorm: Harm Reduction Programs and Interventions

How many and what types of harm reduction programs, approaches and/or strategies can you identify that have been helpful in your outreach efforts with vulnerable populations?

Here's a helpful hint: Take a moment to reflect on the different referrals you have made to harm reduction programs, as well as specific client interventions you have utilized to reduce harm and promote safety.

Discussion

Harm Reduction strategies can begin as early as the initial outreach and engagement process allows. This may depend on the particular service you provide, as well as who is deemed eligible and/or ready for your services. The staff working at various programs, clinics, and/or outreach teams receive orientation and training that often institutes treatment bias. Biases may be encountered due to practical reasons in regard to maintaining sufficient caseloads for billing purposes, or for other less evident reasons such as judging who is most ready or even deserving of a service, among others. This amounts to directing available resources and services to the folks who actively raise their hands and admit to having difficulties and/or issues they need to actively address. Unfortunately, treatment bias often leaves the most vulnerable behind.

By definition, we are taking a Harm Reduction approach when directing our health care and/or outreach services to those who are pre-contemplative, yet clearly present with complex and multiple needs in regard to homelessness, major mental health and/or addiction issues. Our premise is that establishing person-centered relationships are healing opportunities that set the stage for further observations, assessments and interventions that can make people healthier and safer. As noted earlier, some of the need items we provide may also facilitate further engagement, while also decreasing harm to the individuals we serve. Examples range from providing food, water, and camping supplies to distributing condoms.

Our willingness to meet up with folks who are often intoxicated or high on various substances is done in an effort to establish trusting relationships and productive dialogue, so that harm reduction strategies and referrals can be more fully explored. Many of our referrals are to harm reduction services such as needle exchange programs, Narcan training and supplies, so that people sleeping rough can intervene to avert the death of their friends due to overdose. Other examples are Methadone clinics and Suboxone groups that provide Medication Assisted treatments for opioid addiction. Through outreach and partnerships with healthcare providers, we are also able to help folks access Street Medicine teams and/or Health Care for the Homeless services so that their health can be monitored and evaluated on a more regular basis. For example, this can begin by referring a person with complex and multiple medical and psychological needs to a Health Care for the Homeless nurse for something as basic as a foot soak. Hopefully, early positive interactions with healthcare professionals establish trust and may lead to the acceptance of further medical evaluation and treatment.

Similarly, we make referrals and support transitions to "safe spaces" whenever possible. This may include connecting someone who is living outside and actively using drugs and/or alcohol to a shelter that is behaviorally based, and thereby allows folks entry as long as they don't cause conflict with others, or actively use while on the premises. Other examples are placement into housing first programs ranging from Safe Havens with 24/7 staff availability for people with untreated mental illness, and placing others in an independent apartment with wraparound support services that are welcoming, person-centered, and follow Pretreatment principles of care. This is done as part and parcel of a harm reduction approach, as opposed to programs with historical and embedded treatment bias that require sobriety or mental health treatment prior to shelter and/or housing placement.

The measure of our success in Harm Reduction approaches is not only in reduced healthcare expenditures for emergency care, inpatient stays, or lives saved, but also by facilitating further engagement and ongoing safety assessment of those who are most vulnerable. Many of our efforts result in people with complex and multiple needs eventually taking active steps to participate in treatment and recovery services. The following narrative excerpt, questions, and reflections further explore and demonstrate the linkage between harm reduction efforts and initial steps toward recovery.

Example 5-1: Excerpt from Ronald's Narrative (Levy, 2011)

Here, we meet Ronald (B, M, 30s) who has been primarily sleeping rough for several years. Ron would sometimes enter overflow winter shelters, though he could only tolerate these stimulating environments for a few weeks at a time. When I first saw Ron at an overflow shelter, he was isolated from others, smelled of alcohol, and appeared quite pre-occupied with internal thoughts (possibly auditory hallucinations), while muttering to himself. After I observed Ron gesturing with his hands in a manner that seemed nonsensical, I inquired and Ron shared that he was playing "air chess." In response, I joined Ron in a game of imaginary chess. Ron has acumen for chess and enjoyed pretending to move pieces through the air. This established our initial engagement process and Ron eventually (after several weeks) agreed to fill out some housing applications at my office.

The next day I saw Ron sitting and rocking in the waiting area of my office. He appeared oblivious to his surroundings as he laughed and muttered to himself. We immediately started on another housing form, despite my initial inclination to focus on his mental status and asking clinically relevant questions.

This was a judgment call, but I thought it important to deal with the housing issue first, before bringing up other matters. Once the application was filled out, I asked if he had any thoughts on how to establish an income, so he could afford to pay rent. Ron shrugged his shoulders, looked down, and quietly said, "I've bothered you enough. There is no use continuing with this." I quickly replied, "Ron, through my work I've met many people who have felt like giving up, yet eventually we were able to secure income and housing. It may take a little time, but I know that we can do this!" Ron did not immediately respond. Instead, he remained silent, while averting his eyes toward the floor. What he didn't know was that I was a bit taken aback by both his statement and his prolonged silence. I realized that this was part of Ron's pattern of withdrawing from things. Most likely it was his way to avoid uncomfortable topics, which often resulted in him feeling stuck and helpless. My next response was an artful and supportive confrontation to his avoidance. I said, "We can definitely resolve the income issue. I just need your help in figuring out whether it makes sense to find a job or to apply for benefits… Can we figure that out together?" Ron looked up and nodded.

Further meetings followed and it was clear that Ron was not interested in focusing on clinical issues, but was instead inclined toward housing and the need to generate income. As it turned out, our focus on practical income and housing issues resulted in Ron sharing more of his story and my increased understanding of his world.

I now understood that Ron valued his safety and was very conscious of his isolation from others. He presented with significant anxiety, as well as avoidant personality characteristics. This is consistent with a history of trauma. His mental status also showed evidence of a thought disorder. I observed him talking to himself at length on several occasions, though he had never directly confirmed having any delusions or auditory hallucinations. Things were further complicated by his evident addiction to crack and alcohol. While I wanted to get him housed as soon as possible, I was concerned that his level of drug use and psychiatric symptoms would compromise his ability to stay housed and to feel safe with neighbors. The dilemma was that we were considering independent housing options, yet we lacked access to support services and Ron had not yet begun treatment. However, I was aware of a transitional housing program with supports that specialized in homelessness and co-occurring disorders of addiction and mental illness. Figuring that Ron was a good match for this program, I planned to bring this up at our next meeting.

At this point, we had developed a playground of common language. Ron was initially comfortable with the term "un-prescribed medication" as a way to refer to his alcohol and drug use when under stress. He was now empowered to directly discuss his drug and alcohol use inclusive of crack-cocaine. He also expressed a solid vocabulary of mental health terminology such as "anxiety," "stress" and "fear." Finally, I knew that he valued safety, so I planned to frame my offer as a way to feel more secure and less fearful, while waiting for subsidized housing.

As the leaves turned from red and yellow to a uniform brown, we met again at my office and completed applications for income benefits. Upon completion, I asked Ron to consider meeting with folks at a local mental health clinic so he could get some relief from anxiety and stress. I highlighted that this would also help him to secure Social Security Income as quickly as possible. My offer resonated well in Ron's world, so he quickly agreed to the plan. Feeling a bit exuberant by my initial success, I explained to Ron that attaining a subsidized housing placement was most likely a few months away, and so he might feel safer waiting in a more supportive and quieter environment such as a transitional housing program. Ron zeroed in on the word "program" and adamantly refused. He began pulling away before I could even begin to divulge that it consisted of specialized programming for dually diagnosed individuals. At that moment I realized, if we were going to get anywhere, we needed to try independent housing first, and hoped that my misstep would not cost our relationship too dearly.

Over the next two weeks Ron began receiving welfare money and completed an intake at a local mental health clinic that specialized in trauma and anxiety disorders. We began some initial work around strengthening his coping skills, as well as more freely discussing his addiction issues and their impact on his mental and physical health. Within this context, I once again brought up transitional housing with support services as an interim option. I carefully avoided the word "program," while explaining the different mental health and substance abuse services offered. Ronald listened intently before indicating that he appreciated the offer, but was not comfortable attending groups, which he felt would only add to his anxiety. He reaffirmed his need for help, but clearly stated that he was not ready to do more. Although I still wondered if he had a thought disorder and felt concerned about his addiction, I was happy to see him begin outpatient treatment. It took about three months, but we were now off and running with housing applications pending, a source of income established, and pertinent treatment.

On a frigid late November morning, Ron received a letter from the local housing authority requesting an interview and instructing him to bring ID and proof of income. Ron had been offered subsidized housing!

Ron appeared teary eyed and said that he was extremely grateful for all my help. He then looked down and said, "There is something that I should tell you. I am not sure if you will believe me, but I don't feel right keeping it a secret any longer." He then looked up and said, "There's a reason why I've been homeless for so long!" I replied, "You mean something different from what we've already discussed?" Nodding, Ronald continued, "Think of it this way, if you had valuable information... I mean something really valuable like the cure to a deadly disease. What would others do to bring you down?" Bewildered, yet calm, I replied, "What do you mean?" Ron went on to explain, "About five years ago I stumbled upon the cure for AIDS. I can't share too much, but believe me... it's a miraculous cure that's derived from pure sunlight. Now, certain individuals who have some sway with the churches and the police are not happy about this. They've dedicated multiple resources in an effort to silence me. They're involved in nefarious activities meant to bring me down and take away the cure!" I made eye contact and responded, "Ron... I really appreciate how hard it must have been to share such personal details. I am truly taken aback by what you've been going through. My role is to help you to feel safe and to deal with the stress in your life, as well as support your transition to housing. What you shared is really helpful because it gives me a better understanding of your world and your day-to-day challenges." Ron appreciated my response and the session ended with a much greater sense of connection than we'd had through our previous meetings.

The progress we made toward housing played a pivotal role. It opened the door to a greater level of trust and sharing, while also alerting me to what appeared to be a fixed delusional system. Understanding Ron's world, I was able to express, in a sensitive manner, the importance of us sharing at least some of this information with his therapist, so she could help him to manage his stress and anxiety in regard to these issues. I also added that this information may help him to qualify for social security benefits, so we might want to revise his application. In the meantime, he could continue to collect Emergency Assistance money from the department of welfare.

With the New Year rapidly approaching, it had finally happened. Ron not only moved into his own apartment, but he also qualified for social security benefits (SSI/SSDI)! While I was extremely excited to hear the news, this was not the end of our work but a new beginning. Some questions remained:

- Would Ron consistently pay his rent or would his money get spent on drugs or alcohol?

- Would he feel safe and secure in his new apartment or would he end up leaving the apartment due to paranoid delusions?

- Is it safe to move someone with severe mental illness and untreated substance abuse issues into an independent apartment?

Fortunately, Ron remained dedicated to our weekly office visits. Now that he had a safe place to sleep, shower, and shave, Ron looked like he had done a makeover, appearing well groomed and neatly dressed. Further, his recent sharing of his medical research and the plots to bring him down seemed therapeutic. Ron no longer felt alone in his fight for safety and freedom. This level of engagement and trust was critical because Ron could choose to end our relationship and thereby cut himself off from needed support at any time. All he had to do was not answer the door and stop attending appointments. This was independent housing and not part of a program that required ongoing apartment visits or participation in treatment.

During our first meeting at his new residence, we discussed some of the challenges inherent to achieving a stable place to live. Ron clearly understood his responsibilities with paying rent and taking care of his apartment. We also discussed his level of comfort with neighbors and developed a safety or crisis plan in case he ran into any problems. Predictably, major difficulties ensued.

Questions for Consideration

Q1: What harm reduction strategies are utilized by the outreach counselor prior to Ron being housed?

_____

_____

_____

_____

_____

Here's a helpful hint: Think broadly in terms of Pretreatment strategies that may eventually set the stage for treatment, while in the short-term reduce harm by promoting a safe environment or greater preparedness to address potential threats.

Q2: What lessons were learned and how did the counselor recover from the misstep of using the word "program?"

_____

_____

_____

_____

_____

Here's a helpful hint: We have multiple opportunities to identify when we are not in synch with the client in regard to both stage-relevant interventions and Common Language usage. The question is whether or not we are willing and able to adjust our approach.

Q3 How did the counselor utilize a harm reduction approach to melt the "pre-contemplative iceberg" and thereby begin to engage Ron in treatment or recovery-based services?

_____

_____

_____

Here's a helpful hint: Think about the challenges of getting benefits, securing a housing placement and maintaining it. How does this connect with contemplating the need for greater support, counseling, or other types of assistance?

Reflections and Possibilities

The stance of the outreach counselor is to figuratively and literally get where Ron is at and proceed at his pace in order to build trust and strengthen their relationship. Simultaneously, the counselor and Ron have slowly developed a common language to further define their work and the specific goals of generating income and finding independent housing. Over time, this also includes a mental health language that is used to frame out Ron's goal of reducing stress and anxiety by partaking in some outpatient treatment. It is helpful, and perhaps serves as a motivating factor, that the referral for clinical care supports Ron's initial goal of generating income by providing some of the clinical documentation required for SSA or disability benefits. At one point, the worker floats the idea of Ron taking part in a specialized "transitional housing program" for folks with addiction and MH issues, though Ron outright rejects this option as he dislikes the word "program" and sees it as a threat to his autonomy and independence.

The outreach counselor's approach of beginning with Ron's non-clinical goals such as filling out housing applications and then patiently seeing how their work may then connect to clinical considerations is in line with a Harm Reduction approach. This puts the engagement process and establishing good communication first, rather than proceeding too rapidly with clinical assessment and interventions that may compromise relationship development. This allows both the worker and Ron to discover clinical concerns at their own pace and through use of Ron's terminology (Common language construction). Ron is thereby empowered to share his current level of anxiety and his need to do something about it, rather than being diagnosed and directed on how best to proceed without due consideration of his level of engagement and/or readiness for change.

Ron had already begun to self-medicate himself with drugs and alcohol, so this opened the door to discussing other methods that might be more effective at managing anxiety and stress. Having an ear to explore what the client is already doing to manage mental health symptoms and being able to name his illicit drug use as "un-prescribed medication" is a powerful way of moving forward with treatment considerations from pre-contemplation to contemplation (Prochaska & DiClemente, 1982).

Harm reduction strategies (Marlatt & Tapert, 1993) were utilized through relationship building, common language construction, and getting goal centered to slowly melt the pre-contemplative iceberg in regard to both Ron's need for continued illicit drug use and the prospects of receiving mental health counseling to address trauma and anxiety concerns. Most importantly, the outreach counselor's willingness to follow Ron's lead in prioritizing a Housing placement over accessing treatment contributed greatly to the overall success of sustaining a person-centered relationship focused on the goals most relevant to Ron.

This set the stage for housing placement and arguably put Ron in a safer environment than periodically residing at a homeless shelter, or sleeping rough, while grossly intoxicated and experiencing severe symptoms of mental illness. In fact, if implemented with a good support service plan, Housing First *is* a harm reduction approach!

Ultimately, this can be achieved by connecting outreach teams directly to Housing First alternatives to better serve folks with major mental illnesses and/or folks who are dually diagnosed or tri-morbid (medical, addiction, and mental health issues) who are primarily sleeping rough and are not yet ready to participate in treatment (Tsemberis, 2010). The ongoing work to help a person maintain housing often leads to the person taking initial steps toward recovery. This begins by focusing on the universal tasks needed to be successful in an independent housing environment.

These include:

- Paying monthly rent

- Getting along with neighbors

- Taking care of the property

- Basic safety to self and others

- Developing a support network

When working with folks who are often pre-contemplative in regard to clinical issues related to mental illness and addiction, focusing on the above goals in support of the transition to housing often leads to further clinical work as well. It is a very natural process to examine the challenges inherent in achieving the above goals in order to successfully maintain housing. The tenant usually experiences barriers and challenges, and will exhibit behaviors that are discrepant with the above goals. This provides fertile soil for further examination, contemplation and perhaps the beginnings of addressing clinical concerns that interfere with the person's functioning and wellbeing, while being in the safe confines of a residence, as opposed to sleeping outside.

Introduction to Crisis Intervention

This section continues our examination of promoting safety by focusing on crisis intervention, and how this may lead to the opportunity for directly accessing needed treatment and thereby facilitate more rapid positive change. For the purposes of this section, our focus is on psychological crisis, which is defined as psychological duress because our normal strategies of coping and adaption are no longer an adequate fit with environmental/inter-personal demands (Germain & Gitterman, 1980). This causes disequilibrium between the person and environment and intense psychological discomfort that may result in acute states of anxiety, depression, psychosis, etc. Or to put it more concretely, a mental health crisis can be characterized as when a person's normal way of coping and reliance on supports from others hits a brick wall, so they are unable to respond adequately to environmental and interpersonal demands. Further decompensation could lead to the person being an imminent threat to self or others, or inability to provide self-care requiring inpatient psychiatric care to assure safety and wellness. Crisis intervention is not about standing back while the person hurtles toward crisis, then heroically swooping in to "rescue" them. Instead, it is a multi-layered strategy based on engagement, common language, and maintaining a supportive relationship centered on the connections between choices and consequences, and then being there to help the person gain further insights from the crisis. The following exercise, narrative excerpt, questions and reflections will help to further explore the Pretreatment application of crisis intervention.

Exercise 5-2: Personal Exploration of Crisis/Opportunity

Identify a particular crisis in your life that turned out to be an opportunity for growth... How did you get through it and what changed?

_____

_____

_____

_____

Here's a helpful hint: Think about how you managed to survive, what coping strategies and/or supports you relied on, as well as the valuable lessons you learned from the experience resulting in positive change.

Discussion

Throughout our lifetime we are bound to experience points of crisis. Just consider for a moment the natural process of human development and the challenges we may face as we enter our teenage years and again when transitioning from adolescence to young adulthood. Multiple developmental crises are experienced throughout our lifecycle from infancy to old age (Erikson, 1968; Kegan, 1982). Or consider the impact of the passing of a loved one, or the breakup of a meaningful and intimate relationship, or some other significant life event (including violence, mistreatment and/or abuse from others) that may result in significant trauma and/or loss.

It is important to keep in mind that we are "human, all too human," and therefore not immune to life's trials and tribulations. At the same time, each crisis sets the stage for meaningful growth. In this sense, we are all "peers" when it comes to experiencing trauma and loss, managing crises and being deeply impacted by these experiences. In the end, we are certainly more than our traumas, yet our response to trauma helps to mold who we are. Hopefully we can learn from these experiences to become better health care service professionals, outreach workers, counselors, case managers, and peer support staff, etc.

During my adolescent years, my life journey was forever altered by the separation and divorce of my parents, and soon thereafter, the death of my father. He was only 48 years old. Unfortunately, being an adolescent already in the process of pushing away from my mom's authority to achieve a new level of independence (developmental challenge/crisis point) was paired with the family discord that persisted after my parents' divorce. This made it less likely for me to seek support there. The story of my teenage years unfolded with a profound sense of anger and emptiness that quickened my rebellious spirit. My grief and anger were compounded by not being offered the opportunity to attend my father's funeral. Or if it was offered, I was unable to hear it as genuine. The funeral was held out of state and no one seemed willing to take the time or effort to provide support or direction on how to attend. My uncle (father's brother) was the most logical person to take me there, but he was in conflict with my dad prior to his death and was going through his own process of grief and anger. He was remarkably silent on the matter of funeral arrangements and did not offer to bring me there. I felt alone. In many respects, I was at a crossroads with one path heading more toward healing and wellness, versus continued pain and anger that endangered my immediate health and future.

I remember hearing the news of my dad's death and immediately feeling that I had been set adrift. I then roamed the streets of my neighborhood, just hoping to get into a fight. I no longer cared about my own wellbeing, let alone others. Fortunately, I was able to get through the confusion and emotional tumult that immediately followed without major incident. The support of my friends, as well as my active participation in school sports at just the right time, were crucial. Being part of a wrestling team gave me a mission to be the best wrestler I could be. This provided direction and support throughout my grieving process. My daily exercise routine of running ten miles and lifting weights was a desperately needed outlet for my anger and sadness. I can still remember dedicating my wrestling matches to my father's memory, which made my pursuit of "doing the best I can" all the more driven with a sense of purpose.

Tragedies and challenges from my adolescent years led to closer friendships, and provided me with a window into the psychology of grief and loss; the importance of social support, coping strategies, meaningful structure and being part of something larger than oneself that can provide a sense of purpose. Hard lessons learned helped to develop resilience and greater empathy toward myself and others. This resulted in greater self-reflection and independence. In fact, it is impossible for me to separate who I am and what I value from my life experiences of trauma and loss. My interests in philosophy, Narrative Psychology, and the quest to help others are a direct result of my upbringing, culture, meaningful relationships, as well as my early experiences of trauma and loss.

At the same time, it does not feel like these early successes were something earned, but rather they just happened. I had the gift of a strong foundation of love and early connection with my mom, which in many ways was like a blind man's cane seeing me through the turbulent times of trauma and loss. I was fortunate to have the support of friends and family at the right time, while also attending a school that offered me the opportunity to be on the wrestling team. I had the benefit of good health, and a psychology that provided resilience during adversity.

Over the years, I have met so many who have experienced far more extreme incidents of trauma and loss, with fewer supports and opportunities for growth. Unfortunately, many people have significant Aversive Childhood Experiences (high ACE scores) compounded by multiple traumas throughout their lives. So perhaps the greatest lesson learned is to have a deep appreciation for what so many of us who are truly fortunate take for granted such as strong early connections with family, basic health, warmth, friendship, and the healing power of meaningful relationships.

Hopefully, our personal experiences with crisis/opportunity can help us to meet the challenges of promoting client safety, while seeking pathways to positive change. Next, we rejoin Ron and the outreach counselor on their tumultuous journey to greater stability.

Excerpt from Ronald's Narrative (Levy, 2011) – Part 2

Ron showed up at my office and appeared distraught. He handed me a letter he had just received from Social Security. It stated that he needed a payee and was not allowed to directly receive his funds. I had originally recommended this because establishing a payee guaranteed rent payment, while limiting the amount of money that could be spent on drugs and alcohol. Ron did not agree with this recommendation, but we were still able to make a plan on how to institute a payee and I promised to help him devise a budget that would include a weekly spending allotment. I also highlighted that we could get a doctor to sign off on his ability to manage his own funds, but that was not apt to succeed unless we addressed the level of his drug and alcohol intake.

Over the next two months, Ron reported major problems with unwelcome houseguests and his mental status had significantly deteriorated. He still showed up regularly for our appointments, but he was often inebriated, as well as more withdrawn and depressed. Further, he was now willing to discuss his alcohol and drug intake in more detail, but unwilling to consider going to a detoxification facility. Ron stated that he would be far too anxious dealing with groups or being confined to a unit. His treatment team via the local mental health clinic had recently begun Ron on a trial of psychotropic medications. These meds were prescribed to help level out Ron's mood and to alleviate psychotic symptoms, but did little to reduce his social anxiety. Ron experienced these medications as a major step toward reducing stress and helping him to sleep through the night. He also agreed to continue counseling sessions that focused on enhancing his coping skills, as well as

> Our personal experiences with crisis/opportunity can help us meet the challenge of promoting client safety, while seeking pathways to positive change.

developing cognitive-behavioral techniques for reducing stress. However well intended, the effectiveness of this treatment approach was severely hampered by Ron's continued dependence on crack and alcohol. Similarly, our efforts to transition him from homelessness to housing were about to hit a serious roadblock.

Early one morning Ron arrived at my office, and with a sense of urgency asked to meet. He appeared a bit gaunt and was grasping a letter in his trembling hands. It was a letter of eviction for disturbing his neighbors and for illegal drug use. Ron then went on to express, with considerable shame and frustration, how out of control things had gotten. Over the past month his drug use had dramatically increased, and the people distributing the drugs began staying at his apartment throughout the day and sometimes overnight. When they were in his apartment, they would play loud music, get high and eat his food. He was afraid to share this with anyone due to the continued threats of retribution. If he kept the door locked and refused to let people in, they just kept on knocking throughout the night. Due to the continuous loud noise, his neighbors called the police. When the police arrived they cleared the apartment of unwelcomed guests, but also gave Ron a notice to appear in court for drug possession, which was not on his person, but nevertheless in his apartment. Fortunately, he was not immediately put in jail, but now had to respond to a court summons.

Ron, who had successfully avoided the police and others for so long, was in a real fix. He could no longer "not be a bother" by simply avoiding others. He was now forced to confront things in court or lose his housing and go to jail.

Remarkably, in Ron's mind the unwelcomed houseguests and the police had conspired against him. He thought that they worked for a wider network of powerful people who were assigned to discredit him and his cure for AIDS, so pharmaceutical companies could continue to profit by selling drugs to chronically ill people. This resulted in Ron and I discussing ways to better assure his safety and how continued drug use left him confused, defenseless and an easy mark for others to target. The present context of a pending eviction interpreted through the lens of a paranoid delusion jibed well with his need to think clearly so he could better defend himself. In that moment Ron had connected to the discrepancy between his overindulgence on drugs and his ability to remain safe.

Hoping to build some further motivation and gumption, I stated, "Ron, if you want to keep your apartment and stay out of jail, then you need to prove that you are actively addressing these issues noted in the letter." What I recommended was for Ron to enter a detoxification facility that specialized in dual diagnosis issues, followed by a step-down or transitional program. I mentioned that I knew the staff at the detox and they would be sensitive to his level of anxiety. Ron was now contemplative, but wanted time to think things over. We planned to meet the next day.

The following morning, Ron showed up at my office uncharacteristically early and was carrying a small black backpack full of clothes. Before I could say a word, Ron said, "I am ready to go!" We then made arrangements to get him into a detoxification program for dually diagnosed individuals. Even though Ron struggled with his anxiety on a daily basis, he managed to stay twelve full days. He left the detoxification facility in time to attend his court hearing. Because this was Ron's first offense coupled with his recent completion of a detoxification program, the judge was persuaded to continue the case for six months without a finding. The judge stated that Ron needed to report back to the court without any new charges, as well as clear evidence of sobriety. If Ron succeeded, then the charges would be dropped.

Unfortunately, the housing authority was not as sympathetic. They stated that Ron needed to leave the premises, or he would end up in housing court. Upon receiving this news Ron took off and began drinking heavily for several days. Approximately one week later, I knocked on Ron's apartment door and he agreed to meet. He appeared depressed and close to tears. He was now at a crossroads where every decision carried the full weight of major life consequences.

I said, "Ron, it's not too late to turn things around. We have the opportunity to get your court case dismissed!" Ron sadly replied, "What's the difference, if I am going to lose my housing." In an attempt to revive hope, I said, "If you were to voluntarily leave this apartment, we can apply for a future housing subsidy, but if you don't then we will lose that opportunity. I know of transitional housing options that will help you gain sobriety, while addressing issues of stress and anxiety. Not only would you get away from people who have tormented you, but you could graduate from a transitional residential setting to independent housing placement." Ron appeared to be listening as evidenced by his looking up and renewing eye contact. He then weakly said, "I guess we can give it a try." Reassuringly, I responded, "This will look great in the eyes of the court and could qualify you for a new housing subsidy."

After careful deliberation, Ron was willing to enter a transitional residence for people with co-occurring disorders. This meant that he needed to once again enter a detoxification facility, because the transitional residence, which was relapse tolerant, required initial sobriety upon entrance. Ron now knew that he was capable of completing the detox and understood that his future housing and freedom were at stake. He therefore entered a detox facility and transitional residence without major objection.

He spent six challenging months at the transitional residence. We continued to meet weekly at my office with the goal of helping him to adjust, as well as to consider future housing options. For the most part, Ron maintained his sobriety, though he contemplated leaving the residence on several occasions due to his perceived mistreatment by staff. Upon Ron's request, I stepped in on more than one occasion to serve as a mediator. My role was to help Ron and the staff to better understand each other's worlds, language, and values. In the end, Ron not only completed the transitional residential program, but his court case was also dismissed. In addition, he found a self-help group he really liked at the local Social Club program (Clubhouse model) that served adults with major mental illnesses.

Ron accepted a referral to the Department of Mental Health in order to attain permanent subsidized housing with ongoing support services. The support service consisted of monthly case coordination and a weekly home visit. Once affordable housing with community-based supports was fully in place, Ron and I agreed to formally end our working relationship. We decided to celebrate all that had been accomplished with a game of chess. Ron was ecstatic to see me pull out a chess set from my bottom desk drawer. We spent the next hour discussing and playing chess. Ron won the match and left our meeting smiling from ear to ear.

Questions for Consideration

Q1: What points of Crisis/Opportunity can you identify via the above excerpt?

_____

_____

_____

_____

_____

Here's a helpful hint: Consider the need for Crisis intervention in regard to clinical and housing concerns.

Q2: What specific crisis intervention strategies are utilized by the outreach counselor?

_____

_____

_____

_____

_____

Here's a helpful hint: Think in terms of Pretreatment strategies and interventions that facilitate contemplation of treatment options.

Reflections and Possibilities

Upon completion of the homeless outreach process, a new chapter of our work begins with the challenges of housing stabilization. It is helpful to think of our work as a journey. In many respects it is an unfolding story that we are fortunate to witness and hopefully have a positive impact on its flow. At any given point a crisis may arise that is pregnant with the seeds of positive change.

Our work was initially organized around the non-clinical issues of paying rent, getting along with neighbors, and taking care of the apartment, though this quickly morphed into the problem of "unwelcomed house guests" and police intervention. It was a housing crisis that expedited our clinical focus. This resulted in Ron experiencing major anxiety coupled with increased substance use, as well as significant trauma and a profound sense of feeling that everything was out of his control. Not only did Ron fear eviction, but he was also worried about ending up in jail.

If I wanted to be successful in helping Ron access needed treatment, then I also needed to appreciate the organizing force of his delusions. Ron's purpose and sense of meaning were derived from his belief system. Rather than simply diagnosing and medicating, which was not a real possibility at this juncture, I carefully developed a common language that did not conflict with his world. In fact, things were taken a step further by integrating his belief system into my choice of words and concepts to serve as an additional motivation for change. My intervention, which put a high value on our jointly shared concern for safety, asked him to consider the degree to which his drug use had interfered with his ability to keep himself safe from others.

This approach empowered Ronald to contract for detoxification services because he had realized that his illicit drug use and intoxication put his apartment at risk and made him an easy target for others to seize upon, as well as forcing him to appear in court to plea for his freedom. Substance abuse treatment now had a new meaning in his world. Instead of being a "program" that threatened his autonomy, it became a doorway toward safety and future housing stability.

It was during these moments of crisis that important insights were reached and life-changing decisions were made within the confines of a safe and trusting relationship. A Housing First approach provided Ron with the opportunity to learn by doing and sometimes failing, as opposed to being indefinitely stuck or stymied. This approach gave him (maybe his first) reason to trust the systems that are set up, but so often fail, to help. After approximately ten months of working together with me, Ron entered a residential program with a new-found understanding of the importance of achieving sobriety, even if a true sense of recovery still eluded him.

Interestingly enough, this was the same "program" I had suggested many months prior. Back then, Ron did not have the motivation and I did not have the leverage to convince him otherwise. It was a series of crises that provided the opportunity for positive change. Over time, our relationship grew and the words, ideas, and values associated with treatment and recovery were no longer foreign or threatening.

Undoubtedly, my willingness to house him first, rather than insist on residential treatment programs, played a central role in establishing a trusting relationship, as well as helping Ron to understand that I respected his autonomy. This provided a positive and safe relationship for jointly considering restricted options set forth by the courts and housing authority. Only, this time he wasn't alone and homeless. Together, we could face these crisis points with the hope of a better future.

If you are interested in the complete telling of Ronald's story and its implications for Housing First, it is available in the training booklet *Homeless Outreach & Housing First: Lessons Learned* (2011).

References

Erikson, E. H. (1968). *Identity: youth and crisis*. New York: Norton.

Germain, C. B. & Gitterman, A. (1980). *The life model of social work process*. New York: Columbia University Press.

Kegan, R. (1982). *The evolving self: Problem and process in human development*. Cambridge, MA: Harvard University Press.

Levy, J. S. (2011). *Homeless Outreach & Housing First: Lessons Learned*. Ann Arbor, MI: Loving Healing Press.

Marlatt, G. A. & Tapert, S. F. (1993). *Harm Reduction: Reducing the risks of addictive behaviors*. In J. S. Baer, G. A. Marlatt & R. J. McMahn (eds). *Addictive behaviors across the life span: Prevention, treatment, and policy issues (pp. 243-273)*. Newbury Park, CA: Sage.

Prochaska, J. O. & DiClemente, C. C. (1982). Trans theoretical therapy: Toward a more integrative model of change. *Psychotherapy: Theory, Research, and Practice. 19(3): 276-288*

Tsemberis, S. (2010). Housing First: Ending homelessness, promoting recovery and reducing cost. In I. Ellen & B. O'Flaherty (eds) *How to House the Homeless*. New York: Russell Sage Foundation.

6 Facilitating Change: The Art of Enhancing Motivation and Gentle Confrontation

Introduction

The fifth principle of the Pretreatment model is Facilitating Change. This is the last to be addressed, because in many respects the other four principles set the stage for the change process to yield positive results. It is only through the development of a safe and trusting relationship, good communication, and respect for client autonomy that the worker can facilitate the change process. Our Pretreatment work is person-centered and goal focused. The goals we work on are always framed and defined through the client's language. Ultimately it is based on their world and what they value in order to promote a sense of ownership and initiative toward reaching one's goals. Once the contracting stage of the engagement process is underway, the lessons from the change model take on added significance and serve as a valuable guide. While it is helpful during relationship formation to understand the stages of the change with an emphasis on "Pre-contemplation," it becomes a larger component of our approach as our work progresses toward developing goals and achieving positive outcomes.

While many people with insight and problem recognition raise their hands to access traditional modes of treatment, many of the folks we serve lack interest or initially refuse treatment or recovery-based options for healing. A central question for us to ponder is how to most effectively serve those who are squarely within the Pre-contemplative stage of change. In other words, how do we go about melting the "pre-contemplative iceberg?"

Four Pretreatment Strategies to Promote Positive Change

First, it is essential to develop a client-centered relationship that respects the client's autonomy by reinforcing that people are experts in their own worlds. This embraces Jean Paul Sartre's declaration (1956) of the inescapable connection between freedom of choice and responsibility. Upholding choice within the presence of a safe relationship ensures that people are more likely to own their successes, while also being open to reviewing their missteps or mistakes with someone who engenders their trust. In this manner, client-centered relationships empower people to learn the valuable life lessons of what works and what doesn't by instituting a trusted feedback loop between outreach counselor and client, and thereby encourage more responsible choices in the present and near future. This is in accord with a solution-focused approach to helping (Walter & Peller, 1992), which emphasizes our ability to construct present day solutions based on what's worked, while letting go of strategies that have not panned out in the past or present.

Second, we can help people prepare for positive change by focusing on their aspirations, values, wants and needs in order to better define their objectives, and then jointly breaking them down into a step-by-step process of achievable goals. It is important that our work becomes goal-centered and optimistic, rather than problem-centered and defeatist. This is in agreement with the Solution Focused approach (Walter & Peller, 1992), and psychiatric rehabilitative principles of care (Anthony et al., 1990). Psychiatric Rehabilitation is goal focused and thereby defines barriers to change, while understanding the importance of developing and/or enhancing skills, building a strong support system, and modifying the environment as necessary in order to achieve one's goals.

Third, there are a number of ways that gentle confrontation may lead to greater insight. This can provide motivation to move toward change, rather than maintaining entrenched behaviors that have led to negative consequences, a sense of "stuckness," or feelings and thoughts associated with learned helplessness. The process of joining with the person to consider the impact of natural consequences to one's actions is critical. For example, a formerly homeless tenant approached her housing support counselor and shared that she had received a thirty-day notice of eviction from her landlord. The counselor's response to the thirty-day notice for not paying rent may consist of reflecting back the tenant's concern of potentially getting evicted, and then jointly problem solving on how to better address these issues going forward to avoid further negative consequences. Critical to the success of this intervention is joining with the client's words, as well as her anger and frustration, so that it is clear that the eviction letter is coming from an external source. This sets up an "us connection" that jointly explores workable solutions to the problem in a manner that engages the pre-frontal cortex toward problem solving, rather than triggering fight/flight behaviors of argumentation and/or avoidance that's directed at the housing support worker.

In Change Model and Motivational Interviewing language, this includes jointly identifying discrepancies between one's goals, values, and aspirations with current or recent behaviors that are counter to these ideals. Utilizing gentle confrontation, the tenant's fear of eviction can be recast as her aspiration to remain successfully housed and this can lead to some exploration in regard to discrepant behaviors (budgeting issues, giving away money, addiction expenses, etc.) that mitigate paying rent in a timely manner. Our hope is to set the table for greater ownership of workable goals, thereby increasing motivation for positive change. Another helpful technique is to highlight ambivalence and to encourage contemplation for change by giving voice to the different parts of the person, such as the conflict between wanting to successfully maintain an apartment versus the drive to continue to spend money on drugs and/or alcohol that could have been set aside for rent. If a safe non-judgmental space is provided via a trusting relationship, this may encourage a self-inventory where the different parts of the person are given voice to weigh the pluses and minuses of continuing certain behaviors. In this manner, the healthier part of the person can be activated by amplifying the client's ambivalence to consciousness for greater consideration and thereby improve internal communication in an effort to better address ambivalence and resolve internal conflict. This is paired with support, enhancing coping strategies and skill development to empower change.

Fourth, we prefer to join with the person on their quest for change, rather than allowing people to feel alone, isolated, overwhelmed, and powerless. This means that our counseling role goes well beyond standard office-based clinical practice. For instance, we may actively offer to accompany people to attend critical appointments, jointly fill out needed paperwork for housing and other resources, and being there to review their strengths, challenges, and barriers to change. We can further facilitate the change process by getting feedback from the client on the rate of transition, so we don't make the error of moving too quickly based on our own need to promote a change agenda. In fact, many people without homes have complex needs, so their focus on what is of immediate importance may change quickly and without the counselor realizing the need to shift focus. It is important to check-in with clients by reviewing past work and stated goals, as well as inquiring as to where they are at today. Our clients will benefit by our flexibility to respond to immediate needs and construct new goals, rather than adhering to action plans that no longer apply to their most pressing concerns. Joining with the client means that they dictate the pace and substance of the agenda as long as it doesn't conflict with the stated boundaries of our role.

Through our many years of "hands-on" outreach counseling practice, my staff and I have found that utilizing these four Pretreatment strategies improves the chances for facilitating positive change.

Stages of Change and Motivational Interviewing Principles

Prochaska and DiClemente's Trans Theoretical Model of Change (1982) is an important guide. It breaks down the change process into distinct stages to help guide interventions:

- **Pre-contemplation:** Prior to the development of understanding that change is needed

- **Contemplation:** Awareness of problem; ambivalent feelings about change

- **Preparation:** Initial movement away from ambivalence and toward action resulting in preparation for change

- **Action:** Attempts toward achieving change; Implementation of action plan; Steps are made to attain goal(s)

- **Maintenance:** Sustaining the change accomplished by previous actions

- **Relapse:** Previous problem behaviors are repeated resulting in regression to a previous stage such as Pre-contemplation or Contemplation Stages

It is important to note that relapse is expected to be part of the change process, and so a client's movement through these stages is often not linear. Therefore, even after notable progress, it is not unusual for a person to regress back to an earlier stage. Further, someone can be in different stages of change in regard to different types of problems or need areas. I find it particularly useful to think in terms of six different major domains from which to consider what Stage of Change someone currently resides in, and thereby intervene accordingly. They are Addiction, Mental Health issues, Medical concerns, Generation of Income, and the Development of Meaningful Structure, as well as addressing Housing needs. For example, a person can be in the Action Stage of Change in regard to Income and/or Housing, while still Pre-contemplative in regard to Addiction and/or Mental Health issues, and perhaps Contemplative for Medical concerns. The key is to facilitate a person's movement through the stages of change by beginning where they are at and providing the right environment (social and physical safe spaces) to help enhance motivation.

Motivational Interviewing is a well-researched, effective counseling approach that is sensitive to "where people are at," and joins with the person to identify the need for change and promote a sense of ownership over the process. In this manner, it is person-centered and helps facilitate people's movement through the Stages of Change. The hope is to help our clients to enter the Action Stage of change and to eventually achieve and maintain positive life change. The "action" embarked upon by a person experiencing homelessness can range from something as basic as connecting with a nurse for foot care to beginning Mental Health and/or Addiction treatment, or attending to the concrete need of filling out housing applications or promoting housing stability.

Five general principles guide the practice of *Motivational Interviewing* (Miller & Rollnick, 1991, pp. 55-62):

- **Express Empathy:** Skillful reflective listening and joining with the person in need is fundamental. Accept and understand a person's perspective without necessarily agreeing with it. Identify ambivalence, and explore the different parts of the person by giving voice to inner conflict.

- **Develop Discrepancy:** Reflecting on discrepancy between present behavior and a person's stated goals, values, or wishes can motivate change. The client can develop an improved awareness of actions and related consequences, thereby reinforcing personal responsibility for meeting one's goals, or re-evaluating what they need to work on.

- **Avoid Argumentation:** Avoid power struggles. Arguments are counterproductive. Describe rather than label, understand resistance, but don't fight it.

- **Roll with Resistance:** The client is the key resource for creating solutions. New perspectives are jointly considered but never imposed. Resistance is a signal to change strategies.

- **Support Self-Efficacy:** Our counseling approach should be optimistic. Belief in the possibility of change and restored or new-found hope are important motivators. We know that it is beneficial for people to take ownership (personal responsibility) of the change process by actively participating and planning future steps.

These theories (Change Model and Motivational Interviewing) can guide human service workers by providing stage-based interventions to facilitate the change process. The Change Model and Motivational Interviewing can help a person move from Pre-contemplation toward Action in order to become an agent toward creating positive change in their life. Stage-based interventions include, but are not limited to, providing education, facilitating ongoing self-inventory at every phase, and developing structure to support change (e.g., relapse prevention). Further, this approach shows that pointing out discrepancy and thereby creating ambivalence and/or awareness of internal conflict (Contemplation stage) are important positive steps toward addressing issues of denial, or minimization of problems. Therefore, counselors should carefully facilitate some exploration of ambivalence, rather than avoiding this issue. The following Exercise and Example will provide us with the opportunity to further understand and explore the varied applications of the Change process throughout our work, and our role as a facilitator.

Exercise 6-1: Self Reflection on the Change Process

Think about a time in your life when you attempted to change your own behavior or actions in order to achieve a desired goal. Describe your motivation(s) for change and the challenges or barriers that you faced. What approaches or strategies worked and what didn't work?

_____

_____

_____

_____

_____

Here's a helpful hint: This may include common goals such as increasing exercise or losing weight, or trying to be disciplined at learning a new skill such as playing a musical instrument, or more complex challenges such as working on one's recovery from an addiction.

Discussion

Our attempts to foster change is a challenge that each of us face at one time or another. Whether we are trying to end a bad habit with unhealthy consequences, or attempting to achieve an aspirational goal, our focus is on self-improvement. The change process is universal in nature. It begins with first recognizing a problem or bringing to consciousness concerns or issues in need of change.

If you were able to complete this exercise, then you already had some insight rooted in the past and/or present and recognized the need for self-improvement. In other words, you were not pre-contemplative, but already preparing for change or even striving to make it happen. If you were able to meditate on what worked versus what didn't work toward fostering change, then you clearly were in an action phase fueled by some sense of motivation to do better. Where did that motivation come from?

Was it from some internal sensibility instilled through your upbringing based on what you value or find to be of great importance? Or, is it a bit more external? Perhaps it is connected to the circle of family, friends and acquaintances you spend meaningful time with, or a larger community in which you actively participate? After taking a self-inventory and recognizing a personal concern in need of change, what was helpful toward reaching your goal(s)?

Certain strategies are worth mentioning that may facilitate the change process:

- Build a Trusted Support System to provide encouragement and critical feedback

- Share your commitment to achieve a positive change with others who you trust

- Enhance Coping Skills to handle the stress that accompanies attempts to change

- Become Goal Centered and measure progress toward goals by taking a daily personal inventory of progress

- Break down larger goals into smaller, reachable goals

- Reward yourself for any noted progress and take time to celebrate your larger achievements

- Embrace and repeat particular behaviors and strategies that have helped to yield positive results

- Disregard strategies or approaches that have not worked in the past and present

- Connect Change Process to a deeper meaning connected to your values, aspirations, purpose

- Accept that Relapse is a normal part of the Change Process

- Practice patience, self-care, forgiveness and understanding for your all too human attempts to do better

Does any of the above sound familiar? Chances are you listed at least one of them in response to the last question. One thing is for certain, meaningful change takes a great deal of work and is not easy to come by. It is important that we appreciate the difficulty of the task at hand before expecting others to jump into the Change Process via our standard practice of problem centered or goal driven Action Plans.

Many of the people we serve are afraid to hope. They have experienced so much trauma, disappointment, failure, and mistreatment by others that the sense of shame, guilt, and anger that accompany their fears appear too insurmountable to even begin conversations on what's possible. For these folks, our approach is relationship based, more focused on Harm Reduction and Crisis Intervention as we develop a common language that slowly aligns itself with the words and concepts to help the person contemplate the need for change. We've already presented this reality through the stories of Tracy, Andrew, and Judy, among others. In each, we've shown the power of developing trusting relationships and common language to promote healing, empowerment, and achievement of jointly held goals. Here, we continue our journey with a young adult named Anthony. His narrative, provides us with the opportunity for further exploration with our lens focused on the art of gentle confrontation and building motivation to bring about positive change.

Example 6-1: Excerpt from Anthony's Narrative (Levy, 2013)

I met Anthony at a community meal program in Western Massachusetts. He was a slender, well dressed, 19-year-old white male sitting alone with his legs crossed and carefully attending to his soup and sandwich. Upon my approach, he greeted me with a half-smile, while gazing down at his food. We spoke for a short while and he revealed with a slightly anxious voice that approximately one year ago, shortly after graduating from high school, he had a major conflict with his mother and was forced to leave his home.

When I asked him how he gets by without much income or a place to live, he explained that he received welfare benefits, even though he would prefer to work. Where he resided was much more complicated. At first, he stayed in a local motel, but after two weeks he depleted all of his savings. He then enrolled in Job Corps, a residential youth vocational training program, but didn't make it past orientation. After couch surfing for a few months, Anthony stayed a couple of months with a relative, but was asked to leave after they had a heated argument.

I purposely steered our initial conversation away from the content of his interpersonal difficulties and instead explained that I was a Homeless Outreach worker who may be able to help him find a safe place to stay. At that point, Anthony made direct eye contact and in a stern voice said, "One thing you should know is that I am gay, and if you can't deal with that, then I don't need your help!" Surprised, but with well-learned lessons from my past, I responded: "I'm here to help you and I promise to respect who you are, while doing my best to help you achieve your goals."

I knew of a small shelter whose supervisor was openly gay. I described the shelter, which fit the description of a rundown quaint house, and the openness of the staff to serve people from all walks of life. Furthermore, the shelter only served up to 16 men and women at a time, which made the environment reasonably quiet and private in comparison to larger shelters. Anthony immediately showed interest and I was able to facilitate placement that same evening.

I left our meeting concerned about whether or not Anthony would be successful at following the rules of the shelter, as well as his ability to get along with others. As it turned out, Anthony had a long trauma history consisting of numerous beatings by his step-dad, and was furthered wounded by his mother's inability to embrace his gay identity. Worse than that, she was directly hostile to his sexual orientation and this led to his departure from his childhood home into the uncertain world of young adulthood. This history of trauma in conjunction with the developmental stage of young adulthood often leads to questioning and rejecting authority, as well as general difficulties with establishing acceptance among one's peers. An additional layer that further complicates matters was that someone who is gay will encounter very real biases and abuses that could put their health and safety at risk, while posing a direct challenge to their search for intimacy and developing a sense of belonging.

Understandably, Anthony was very sensitive to any perceived mistreatment from others and this set in motion a dynamic that invariably led to interpersonal conflict. Any sense of disrespect, including when staff told him to do a household chore, rather than a polite inquiry, caused Anthony to go into a rage. This consisted of belligerent language followed by him storming off to his shelter bed or leaving the shelter, while shouting expletives. Unfortunately, a couple of the shelter guests fed into these negative behaviors by taunting him with derogatory and abusive slogans that belittled him for being gay, such as "Once again, the little fagot is having a hissy fit." I share this not to be crude, but to make readers aware of the cruelty Anthony was forced to endure.

I consulted with staff on how best to respond to Anthony's acting-out behaviors, while also advising them to set strong limits on hate speech by other shelter guests. Fortunately, the shelter supervisor was very empathic to Anthony's plight and responsive to my feedback. This resulted in the shelter manager making and immediate declaration of a zero-tolerance policy for hate speech in regard to race, religion, creed, color, sex, age, gender identity, and sexual orientation. This was clearly posted on the wall, with an understanding that violation of this policy would mean an immediate warning and possible dismissal from the shelter.

Solution Focused Work: Crisis Intervention and Contracting

A short time later, I caught up with Anthony and he was less communicative and appeared hesitant to engage. Sensing this difficulty, and instead of immediately focusing on the turmoil that had just transpired, I invited him to come join me for a cold beverage at a local cafe. After all, it was ninety degrees outside and Anthony needed a break from the shelter environment. Once we were seated and calmly sipping our ice teas, I asked, "What would you like to see happen in your life? I mean... If you had the power to change or do anything, what would it be?" As it turned out, the timing was right and Anthony was ready to talk about his aspirations. He said, "I just want to get away from all the craziness. You know what calms me the most?" As I began to shake my head; Anthony blurted out, "I love to cook! My dream is to own a cafe... just like this one! I could plan the menu and prepare the cuisine, or even manage it. People would come from everywhere just to enjoy my specialties."

At first, I was speechless; this was what we refer to in narrative circles as a "sparkling moment" or a chance to "work with the exception." In other words, Anthony's statement focused on his strengths and dreams, rather than being centered on his problems and deficits. I responded, "That's a wonderful vision! Maybe we can figure out some reachable goals that will get you closer to making that a reality. I recently heard about a job training program that teaches food preparation and cooking skills. I don't remember all the details, but I could look into it for you. If you're willing to work with me, I think I could help." Anthony agreed and we contracted to focus our energies on making his dream an eventual reality.

In fact, I knew of a new culinary arts training program geared toward serving homeless individuals with mental illnesses. It partners with a local MH Clubhouse vocational program, which can provide job coaches and support workers for members who are interested in being certified in food safety and help them to work in the culinary arts field. This allowed students to train in food preparation, so they could assist area chefs at local hotel restaurants, while also providing a subsidized housing placement with ongoing support services. However, I decided to temporarily hold off on sharing this particular resource because I needed to further explain things so Anthony could better understand the role of Clubhouses and not be turned off or feel stigmatized by the label of mental illness. More to the point, I needed to first address some of the significant interpersonal issues that could put this plan at risk.

I said to Anthony, "There is one thing that gets me worried... I really want to see you succeed, yet I am concerned about all of the recent conflicts at the shelter and I get the sense that it's been a real struggle to deal with others... Can you tell me how you look at things?" At that moment Anthony began to share his story of abuse, neglect, and rejection due to his sexual orientation. He understood his rage as righteous anger for being ignored and mistreated. I initially responded by informing Anthony of the recent changes at the shelter to protect him and others from hateful speech. I told him that I certainly respected his right to identify himself as a gay male and so did the supervisor of the shelter, which was one of the main reasons why they instituted the new policy. Those who made hateful remarks have been warned and we wanted to assure his safety and well-being. Anthony was taken aback by all of this and was able to see, at least for the moment, that people really did care. He said, while looking down and close to tears, "I can't believe that they'd do that for me. I am really touched."

At that point we were well engaged, and I could tell that my words had meaning in Anthony's world. A conversational ease was established and I took advantage of this by once again sharing my concerns around the degree that Anthony acts out his anger. I said, "I'm glad you can see that people are making efforts to improve things, but that also puts an onus on you to try and manage how you treat others. Do you know what I mean?" Anthony once again described all the things that got him angry. I gently interrupted and said, "I understand why you get angry and you have every right to your anger, but I am just concerned about the way it gets expressed. It sometimes comes across as just too much... What I mean is that not every disagreeable situation warrants the same type of response." Anthony thought about this for a moment and responded with insight, while also letting me know that he would not tolerate much more on this topic, "If you'd been through what I have been through you'd respond the same way!" To help bring things to a close and to set up future work I said, "You're right about that. I would respond the same way. It isn't your fault that you have been through so much pain. I'd like to help you to manage some of the pain and anger, so you can be more successful in your interactions with others, whether it be at the shelter, or in the future when you're managing your own café." Anthony nodded as the intensity of our ninety-minute conversation began to wane. We left off with a plan to meet again in a couple of days so I could share more information on vocational programs, as well as follow up on developing skills and supports for managing anger and rage. This was a major step in re-constructing Anthony's narrative with concern for interpersonal relations and directly relating it to his future aspirations.

Questions for Consideration

Q1: What was Anthony's "sparkling moment," and how did the counselor set the stage for it to arise?

_____

_____

_____

_____

_____

Here's a helpful hint: Consider the engagement process and stage relevant interventions, as well as how the counselor directly encouraged Anthony to express his interests and what he values.

Q2: How does the counselor use Anthony's "sparkling moment" to reinforce their working relationship and instill motivation for change?

_____

_____

_____

_____

Here's a helpful hint: Consider how Anthony's vocational goal was used to help him contemplate potential barriers to his success and/or related concerns.

Reflections and Possibilities

The counselor's work was twofold. First, it was to remain connected with Anthony, regardless of his outbursts toward others, and help him to appreciate that his exceedingly strong reactions had and would continue to undermine his future prospects. Often, but not always, Anthony responded in a disproportionate manner to someone being disrespectful or lacking sensitivity to his plight. Instead of beginning the conversation with a focus on resolving interpersonal discord, the counselor offered to join Anthony for a cold drink at a local cafe. An informal meeting at the cafe provided a safe space (psychologically and environmentally) for being solution focused, rather than an immediate discussion, and the defensiveness that most assuredly would have followed, about the recent conflict at the shelter. This provided the opportunity for Anthony to have his "sparkling moment." He was empowered to at least fleetingly let go of a narrative centered on mistreatment to one looking forward to reaching his dream of owning a café.

The ability of the counselor to assess and intervene with further engagement strategies, as well as amplifying Anthony's positive striving was crucial toward successfully engaging Anthony in a lengthy and productive dialogue. This consists of helping him to be goal centered, so the preparation stage could begin by planning the steps for positive change. Anthony may then have the opportunity to re-organize his behaviors around attaining these goals. In short, we needed to find a meaningful purpose to help motivate behavioral change, and his desire to manage a café and/or become a chef seemed to fit the bill.

Anthony was now motivated to achieve positive change by being goal focused and having the support of a trusting relationship with the outreach counselor. The outreach counselor was situated as an authentic witness toward Anthony's efforts to achieve his stated vocational objective, while helping him to contemplate barriers and new strategies to promote positive change. This includes gently confronting Anthony by prompting him to take a self-inventory on what's working vs. what's not working toward goal attainment, as well as pointing out discrepancies between his current behaviors and his stated aspirations for further self-reflection and dialogue with the counselor. Directly related to this point was the counselor's efforts to frame Anthony's angry outbursts as sometimes being disproportionate to the matter at hand, and sharing a concern that this could make it more difficult to achieve his dream of being a café owner. Doing this sets the stage for our work on how to better get along with others and stay safe, while also developing the critical skills of conflict resolution and regulating emotions. These are skills that all young adults, including Anthony, need to learn to be successful at work and in life.

At this point in the process, Anthony was able to hear some of this, but was not yet able to participate in productive dialogue that could facilitate deep contemplation on how to best address this issue. While the counselor was on the edge of pushing things too fast, arguably seeds for change were successfully planted.

Excerpt from Anthony's Narrative (Levy, 2013) – Part 2

Two days later I dropped by the shelter and Anthony appeared highly distraught. He was very angry; shown by both his demeanor and the way he was slamming things onto the kitchen counter while he prepared a snack. I calmly walked into the kitchen and asked if anything was wrong. He then went into a rant on how nobody cared about him and how tired he was of this godforsaken shelter. I invited him to speak in private and he agreed to meet in an office that was situated right off the main dining area.

Once we were seated, I asked Anthony if anything was bothering him. He replied, "Nobody wants to talk with me. Now that they got these new rules all I get is the silent treatment and I am not going to stand for it!" I responded, "One of the hardest things is to find acceptance. You are not alone in wanting to be respected, but you can't control what others do. Let's focus on what you can actually do, while being here. Do you know what I mean?" He responded meekly, with a diverted gaze, "You don't know what I'm going through. Last night I felt so down, I just started cutting myself." Anthony then proceeded to roll up his sleeves and revealed some well-aged cuts and scratches on one arm, paired with fresher wounds on the other. None of the cuts looked particularly deep, nor was there any current bleeding, but I was nevertheless alarmed. After a deep breath, I said, "Anthony, when I see all those cuts, I get worried about your safety. Clearly, this is not the first time you've done this. Have you ever gotten any help for this issue?" Anthony shared his history of cutting along with his history of mental health counseling and psychiatry. This included an involuntary inpatient stay when he was sixteen years old. After some further discussion, I remarked: "It sounds like your mood fluctuates a great deal from day-to-day, or maybe even within the same day. I say that because just two days ago we had drawn up a plan around your dream of working and owning a cafe, and now you're letting me know how depressed and empty you can feel... Like there is absolutely no one who cares. Is that a fair statement?" Anthony nodded, and once again went on to explain how often he was mistreated and how angry this made him. After doing my best to reflect back his words and his strong feelings of being hurt and enraged, I said, "There is definitely a relationship between the level of pain that you've experienced throughout your life and the degree of outrage and anger you've expressed. No one can blame you for those feelings, but I still get concerned over how this impacts your ability to interact with others. We need to create a space where you can feel a sense of purpose and belonging, as opposed to spending most of your energy on perpetual conflicts. Does that make sense?" This once again brought the issue back to the here and now, as well as put the ball in his court for action, rather than just feeling stuck and overwhelmed with feelings of despair or rage. Anthony agreed that he would like to see that happen, but was perplexed over what to do or how to begin.

In response to this dilemma and within the context of Anthony's unfolding narrative, we explored meaningful options. I asked, "When you were really upset, where did I find you?" Anthony replied, "I was in the kitchen preparing a snack." I exclaimed, "Exactly! You already know what helps you through some of these feelings... Maybe we could set something up via the shelter supervisor that'd allow you to prepare the nightly snack for shelter guests... Not necessarily every night, but I am sure that they could use a few more volunteers!" For the first time during our meeting Anthony smiled and not only was in agreement, but boasted, "If given a chance, I could definitely improve the snack menu!" Buoyed by Anthony's openness to food preparation and realizing that we had already discussed the concept of mental health via his psychiatric history, I added, "The culinary arts program we spoke about at our last meeting is available via the local Clubhouse where they help people with histories of mental health concerns to focus on recovery and employment. If you're interested, we could set up a tour, so we can learn more about it." Feeling supported and heard, Anthony agreed to the tour and seemed once again excited about his future prospects. Our meeting continued with a safety assessment and Anthony assured me that he felt much better and in control. He shared, "I wasn't trying to kill myself, but I sometimes feel so numb that I don't know what to do."

This led to further contemplation and preparation by formalizing stress and anger management options derived from what had worked for him in the past. In response, we wrote a list of coping strategies down on an index card that he could keep safely in his wallet for future use to avert emergencies. These coping strategies included taking a long shower to promote relaxation, going on short walks to take a break from things, and playing certain songs to help inspire him, as well as doing a fun activity such as cooking. At the very bottom of the card I included and highlighted the number to the local mental health crisis team, which was available 24/7 for assessment, counsel and consult. We left off with a plan to meet the next day, so we could once again review his coping strategies and how to utilize the crisis team, as well as follow up on scheduling the Clubhouse tour and snack preparation via the shelter. It was now evident to me that my work with Anthony during this phase remained quite intensive. My hope was to help him build a support network, so he could practice coping strategies, as well as turn to others when he felt mistreated, rejected, and alone.

The following day I attended a meeting with shelter staff and they were quite thankful for my work with Anthony. I explained to the staff some of the interpersonal difficulties he had experienced, including his struggles for acceptance by others as a young gay man. I recommended that they assign a caseworker who could be supportive around these issues, as well as connect him with a Healthcare for the Homeless nurse who could respond to his medical needs, as well as review HIV/AIDS risk and safe sex practices. Anthony could certainly benefit by having others who he could check-in with on a daily basis. Earl was assigned as his shelter case manager and later that day the three of us met to discuss the topic of shelter snack preparation. This was a perfect way to acquaint Anthony with Earl, as well as to directly connect them with Anthony's goal of cooking for others. Anthony and I also reviewed his newly formulated coping strategies and added Earl and myself as supportive contacts he could turn to for assistance. We expanded the list of coping strategies on the index card that Anthony kept in his wallet with the understanding that whenever it was needed, he could quickly access it for guidance. That night Anthony baked brownies for a shelter snack and it was a big hit. From that day forward, Anthony prepared the shelter snack three times per week and, with Earl's assistance, he even went shopping for groceries. A couple of days later he had his first appointment with Healthcare for the Homeless and it went very well.

The next week, I referred Anthony to the local MH Clubhouse, and within one month's time he began volunteering in the kitchen to prepare a daily free lunch for fellow Clubhouse members. Clubhouses or Social Clubs follow psychosocial rehabilitation principles, as opposed to a medical model of diagnosis, illness and treatment of symptoms. The Clubhouses focus on self-help, friendship, recreational activities, housing, and establishing meaningful and gainful employment, among other things. When working with youth it is extremely helpful to find an environment where they can find a sense of acceptance and community, so I felt very fortunate to secure Anthony a Clubhouse placement that was within walking distance of the shelter.

Questions for Consideration

Q1: What was the nature of the crisis that Anthony experienced at the shelter and how did the worker respond?

_____

_____

_____

_____

Here's a helpful hint: Consider how the worker's response encouraged Anthony to connect with his abilities, strengths, and his stated goal of attending a culinary arts class.

Q2: What enabled Anthony to enter the "Action phase" of addressing mental health issues?

_____

_____

_____

_____

Here's a helpful hint: Consider how crisis can present the opportunity for positive change and how the counselor utilized Pretreatment principles of care. Think about new tools or insights that Anthony developed throughout the outreach counseling process.

Reflections and Possibilities

Anthony had already shown a pattern of struggling with issues of acceptance and being rejected by others. The response by many in the shelter community was to avoid and ignore him, and thereby not have to be responsive to new rules. Unfortunately, Anthony was particularly susceptible to these passive-aggressive behaviors of neglect due to him being a young gay male in search of acceptance and having a significant history of trauma and rejection stemming from his immediate family.

As difficult as this session was, it provided the opportunity for the counselor to embrace crisis and move the work forward toward positive change. Once Anthony showed evidence of his recent cutting behaviors, it provided the impetus for the counselor to show genuine concern and worry, while exploring Anthony's history of mental health care. Psychiatry and mental health considerations were now on the table and their common language had broadened from gay identity issues, past trauma and vocational pursuits, to discussing his mood fluctuations, unstable mental states, and past behavioral health treatment. From there, the counselor adeptly helped Anthony to contemplate what had helped him to cope with these powerful feelings in the past. This led to composing a list of cognitive-behavioral strategies, and also encouraged Anthony to move forward with a plan to cook shelter snacks and enroll in the culinary arts program at the MH Clubhouse.

Anthony, who felt alone and disempowered by lack of acceptance by others, now had a sense of empowerment by reconnecting to his formidable cooking skills and future aspirations of owning a cafe. Within the context of a trusting relationship and a shared common language that respected Anthony's narrative, a referral to a Mental Health Clubhouse and the consideration of future clinical care could resonate in his world. Between active safety planning, accepting shelter case management support, and agreeing to attend an MH Clubhouse program, Anthony had entered the *Action Stage of Change* for addressing mental health needs.

This also brings to the forefront the complex issue of job readiness versus applying for or remaining on welfare or disability benefits. While it is important to work with someone's dreams, it can be difficult to judge a young person's current or potential level of vocational functioning.

When serving young adults with limited work histories and the promise of a long future, it is particularly important to try a myriad of educational/vocational and supportive employment options. Fortunately, there were vocational training programs that are geared toward helping folks with disabilities and are quite savvy on how to achieve an individualized plan that balances the need for benefits with work opportunities. This seemed to be the right path for Anthony, since he was already on welfare benefits, yet had expressed interest in attaining work.

We now had the option of learning about the level of his vocational functioning as we went, while still applying for social security benefits just in case his plan to work was unrealistic. Anthony had subtly embarked upon an experiment to test his vocational abilities. This was yet another way of supporting the process of gentle confrontation, which is rooted in the adage of "learning by doing." In a universal sense, much of life is a grand experiment with no guarantees. The counselor may fall back on this wisdom to express an open mindedness about following the wishes, dreams and aspirations of our clients without judgment. Ultimately, things will sort themselves out through the process of us bearing witness to the client's plight and together contemplating and reflecting on the lessons learned as we go. This stance is more essential than it sounds, as our a-priori judgments are often mistaken. I've witnessed too many miracles, that is, experiments that seemed destined for failure turning into client success stories, to think otherwise. The key is to attain a productive dialogue supported through the practice of Pretreatment Principles of care.

Excerpt from Anthony's Narrative (Levy, 2013) – Part 3

After six weeks of working with Anthony, it was evident that he had made great strides. He had successfully shared his culinary skills with both shelter guests and Clubhouse members, while meeting with Earl and me on a regular basis for case management and outreach counseling services. However, Anthony remained reticent toward getting Mental Health treatment and was growing increasingly impatient with waiting for an opening in the culinary arts training program.

Our newfound success had hit a snag. I received a phone call from a Clubhouse advocate notifying me that Anthony had just stormed off the premises. He reportedly had a major run-in with another Clubhouse member and got angry with the staff when they didn't immediately take his side. I went over to the shelter and Earl (Shelter Case Manager) quickly got my attention and reported that Anthony announced that he was leaving and was currently at his bunk packing up his stuff. I approached Anthony and asked, "What's going on?" Anthony responded in an angry and dejected tone, "I am getting out of here! People just want to take advantage of me and I am not going to put up with it." I responded, "Anthony, I am confused... What just happened? Why are you leaving?" He went on to say that one of the Clubhouse members was bossing him around the kitchen and that everyone was using him to get free meals. He then stated, "Look... I've been cooking and helping out for weeks and still haven't offered a space in the culinary arts program. This is a bunch of bull!" I then noticed that there was some blood slowly dripping down his right arm and I knew that I needed to act fast, so I could assess his safety and hopefully help him to reconsider his current plan.

I said, "I know that when you wait for something it can feel like it's never going to happen and it also sounds like that whatever went on at the Clubhouse really hurts. Right now, you're upset and your arm is bleeding. Let's take a breather and tend to your wounds." Anthony looked down and fell silent. After about 30 seconds, which seemed like an eternity, I said, "Come on Anthony; let's get you some water and bandages, so we can chat." Anthony agreed and we made our way to the bathroom to wash off his self-inflicted wounds. Thankfully, these appeared to be just surface scratches and the bleeding had stopped. Upon our return from the bathroom, I established direct eye contact and said, "Anthony, I'm here for the long haul. Please don't forget that when things get hard, we can talk."

We then spent the next thirty minutes discussing his expectations and the merits of the vocational-food preparation program. I assured him that the culinary arts program and the attached subsidized housing was real, but that it would still take about three to four weeks before they'd have another opening. In the meantime, I offered to set up an orientation meeting with the program case manager who worked at the Clubhouse. He then said in a rapid voice with notable anxiety, "I think I blew it... I don't even know if they will let me back there. I was so enraged that I told off the staff." I responded in a calm and reassuring manner, while using his expressed concern as leverage, "I think that if you went to the local MH Clinic to work on things with a therapist, that would definitely help us to advocate for your return to the Clubhouse." Thankfully, Anthony was on board with that idea.

We then proceeded to talk about his inner struggle or conflict and how that could sap motivation and become a barrier to success. I often frame this as a conflict between the different parts of ourselves. I explained this to Anthony in the following way, "I can clearly see that you're talented, intelligent and that you're really striving to do better, while at the same time another part of you is understandably hurt, angry and impatient. After all, you've been wounded by all the abuse you've been through. Perhaps therapy will help you to better understand these different aspects of who you are and align yourself more fully with your goals." He commented, while slowly shaking his head, "I am so tired of fighting myself and others. At this point, all this conflict is getting in my way. Maybe seeing a therapist will help... I don't know. I certainly appreciate how much you have been there for me." I again responded, "Thank you Anthony... That means a great deal to me. I'll continue to be there for you, but I also want you to have a safe place where you can explore the challenges of being a gay male in a society that isn't very tolerant. Hopefully, you and your therapist can establish the type of relationship where you can comfortably talk about these things." Our session ended with a review of the list of coping strategies, which he kept securely in his wallet. Ironically, when he was pulling the index card from his wallet it exposed a razor blade that was hidden underneath. Anthony then took out the razor blade, held it up in plain sight, and announced, "I don't need this anymore!" as he handed it to me.

As it turned out, Anthony began attending therapy sessions and even agreed to a medication assessment by a psychiatrist, while continuing to receive medical services via Healthcare for the Homeless. His psychiatrist prescribed him Trazodone, which is a psychotropic medication that may help improve sleep, as well as reduce symptoms of anxiety and depression. Anthony agreed to give it a try. In turn, the Clubhouse accepted him back, and within four weeks he began attending classes to earn a culinary arts training certificate and possible job placement. This also led to him being assigned a case manager via the Next Step program. The Next Step program runs in conjunction with the Clubhouse and provides support staff in regard to job training, placement, and coaching services, as well as housing search, placement, and ongoing residential support services. Once Anthony was enrolled in the Next Step program he was awarded a housing voucher (HUD funded) that could be accepted by a landlord to subsidize his new apartment at thirty percent of his income.

None of this was easy. There were several more incidents along the way that mirrored what has already been shared. Regardless of the particular underpinnings and specifics of the crisis or conflict at hand, it was critical for me, as an outreach counselor, to remain available and patient. At times it was akin to navigating and steering through rough seas. It took a steady hand! In this case, I maintained a consistent and accepting presence, while staying on course toward goal attainment.

Since our first meeting, Anthony's support system had grown considerably. It now included Clubhouse members/staff, and a Next Step case manager, as well as his therapist, psychiatrist, shelter case manager (Earl), and me. Anthony consistently attended his vocational training program where he had positive interactions with both the instructor and his classmates. He did well in class and was very proud of his newfound skills and knowledge of safe food preparation. Most impressively, since the day that Anthony gave me his razor blade, there were no further incidents of cutting. It seemed like he had successfully funneled (sublimated) much of his anger away from himself and toward proving that others were wrong about him. He now wanted to succeed, in order to get back at all the people who had sold him short and did him wrong. His anger was now fueling positive change!

After being at the shelter for approximately four months, Anthony was offered subsidized housing with Next Step support services. His move-in date was scheduled to occur within two weeks and we were excited to celebrate his success. Surprisingly, Anthony walked into the common area and appeared to be upset. I invited him to sit down so we could talk, and Anthony shared the following with notable anger: "People can't wait to see me go. Nobody wants me to stay here!" I responded, "Anthony, we're proud of what you've accomplished and we want to celebrate it! I want you to know that we'll miss you. I worked closely with you and I am proud that you are ready to take the next step." After a momentary pause Anthony declared, "I want you and everyone else to know that I don't need or want a celebration!" He then abruptly left the room. Upon his leaving, I was once again reminded of the difficulties many of our clients faced. Anthony and I had forged a significant helping relationship at a very vulnerable time in his life. My expectation for him to be happy about getting housed did not factor in the depth of our relationship and his feelings around loss and rejection. The truth was that over the past month, Anthony could sense my pulling away as others became more central to achieving his future plans. This was purposeful, but I recognized my misstep. We had not spent enough time discussing this gradual, yet steady change in our relationship. "Redefining the relationship" is one of the central tasks of termination and this is particularly important with impressionable youth who lacked parental guidance. In that moment, immediately following my reflection on the difficulties of termination, I was cognizant of the challenges that lay directly ahead.

During the next week, Anthony kept his interactions with Earl and me purposely brief. In response, we decided to try and break the ice with a peace offering that would show how much we valued him and his accomplishments. The next day, after Anthony left the shelter to attend class, Earl and I decorated the common area with streamers and prepared a cake to congratulate him on his achievements. We were also able to get several shelter guests to participate in warmly welcoming him back from school. When Anthony first arrived, he was absolutely shocked! His eyes began to well up with tears, as we all gave him a long round of applause. I then briefly addressed the group. "Anthony, you've shown us a fine example of how to succeed regardless of difficult circumstances. Not only have you continued to do well at school, but in a few days you'll be moving to your own subsidized apartment. Congratulations from all of us!" This was followed by Anthony gladly cutting the cake and he was once again feeling connected. All in all, this was a much healthier outcome than him holding on to the vestiges of pain, anger, and rejection.

Afterward, Anthony and I sat down to meet. We spent the time reviewing his many transitions and successes from first entering the shelter to becoming a Clubhouse member, as well as enrolling in the Next Step Program and participating in a culinary arts training program. We also reviewed the array of ongoing supports and what role each person served from his therapist and psychiatrist to his Next Step case manager. I also reminded him of the razor he'd given me in exchange for his index card of coping strategies. We both knew that it was the nature of our relationship and not the card in and of itself that empowered Anthony to take such a bold step. Yet within the context of termination, the index card served the additional purpose of being a meaningful transitional object that represented both our work and Anthony's hard-earned gains. Together, we recognized that Anthony had shown great courage to walk down the path toward uncertain change.

Shortly thereafter, Anthony moved into his new apartment and continued to get support services through the Clubhouse and Next Step. He successfully graduated from the culinary arts training program and began some food prep work at a local hotel restaurant. A few months later he dropped by to say hello. Near the end of our brief visit Anthony turned to me and said, "I'll never forget all that you've done for me. I did my best to leave on a sour note and you wouldn't have it. I want to thank you for believing in me." I smiled and said, "Anthony, I'll never stop believing in you!" He then shook my hand and headed for the exit. As I made my way back to the meal program where Anthony and I first met, I thought to myself that it's unusual in my line of work to get direct thanks, but this one was well worth the wait!

A fuller account of Anthony's narrative, as well as additional information on youth homelessness can be found in *Pretreatment Guide for Homeless Outreach & Housing First: Helping Couples, Youth, and Unaccompanied Adults* (2013).

Questions for Consideration

Q1: What motivated Anthony to engage in services at the local mental health clinic?

_____

_____

_____

_____

_____

Here's a helpful hint: Consider specific crisis interventions by the counselor that facilitated the Action Stage of Change

Q2: What specific interventions by the counselor helped Anthony to recognize, uphold, and consolidate positive change?

_____

_____

_____

_____

_____

Here's a helpful hint: Consider the different aspects of the termination process between the worker and Anthony inclusive of the challenge of celebrating his success. How did the celebration give Anthony a renewed opportunity to hope?

Reflections and Possibilities

Anthony's story highlights the four Pretreatment strategies for facilitating the change process. First and foremost, the worker develops a person-centered relationship with Anthony that is goal focused. Second, the particular goals worked on have a direct connection to Anthony's aspirations to run or own a café. Third, gentle confrontation is utilized on a number of occasions to point out discrepancies between his immediate goals, values, and aspirations versus how his current behaviors may present barriers to his success. This was also achieved by giving voice to his ambivalence, highlighting the different parts of the person and providing a forum to encourage internal communication and conflict resolution. Fourth, the counselor often joined with the client so they could jointly face and respond to the issues at hand. It was Anthony who dictated the pace and substance of the agenda through his words and actions. So it was up to the counselor to be aware of the current stage of change and the particular issue Anthony was most ready to address.

In this excerpt, Anthony continues to struggle with acceptance/rejection issues and this once again arose during his participation at the Clubhouse Program. The combination of feeling underappreciated for his contribution of preparing meals and waiting for weeks to get into a culinary arts placement proved too much for Anthony to handle. His response was to tell off Clubhouse members and advocates, declare to shelter staff that he was now leaving, and to resume "cutting" behaviors that could compromise his safety.

The outreach counselor immediately responded to this crisis by taking the opportunity to *join* with Anthony and reaffirm their connection by stating, "Anthony, I'm here for the long haul. Please don't forget that when things get hard, we can talk." A reminder of genuine caring by the counselor provided an opening for Anthony to review the issue at hand and potentially get perspective. So, he was able to engage in further conversation in the safe, supportive presence of the counselor, as opposed to being overwhelmed and alone with intense emotions leading to fight, flight, or freeze responses.

It was within this context that the counselor was able to intervene further to discuss the benefits of Mental Health Counseling. Initially this was done by reassuring Anthony that the Culinary Arts Program and the future possibilities it represented were both very real and would soon be available. This helped Anthony to reconnect to his aspirations and immediate goals. He then realized that his most recent behaviors at the Clubhouse put this plan in jeopardy. The counselor was then able to use the feared natural consequences of Anthony's recent interpersonal conflicts as both a leverage point and an opportunity to suggest that therapy may help to smooth things over with Clubhouse staff. Further and deeper contemplation was facilitated when the counselor helped Anthony to connect to the different parts of himself that may at times be in conflict. This consisted of the part of him that feels most vulnerable to rejection and criticism versus the part of him that's more in line with his considerable strengths and vocational aspirations. Therapy was discussed as a chance to further understand these different aspects of himself and how to avoid the pitfalls of allowing his interpersonal struggles to stymie his potential.

This process of deeper contemplation helped Anthony to further embrace the idea of attending a mental health clinic, as it now had much greater relevance to his world, relating directly to his needs, wants, and future goals. His pattern of interpersonal conflict leading to an emotional crisis fueled by a sense of rejection and anger was now becoming more and more discrepant with the part of himself that yearned for success. The witnessing by the counselor and his art of gentle confrontation with Anthony was now yielding positive results. Anthony was now equipped to have a richer inner productive dialogue that gently confronts himself to stay on the pathway toward positive change. In this manner, Anthony entered the Action Stage of Change by agreeing to and then attending therapy and psychiatry sessions at the local mental health clinic.

In time, the counselor was able to successfully involve other services and resources to help Anthony to attain his goals. This included the support of shelter staff, access to treatment via a local mental health clinic, facilitating the connection with Clubhouse services, as well as mediating conflict and restoring these connections with renewed purpose. Anthony also learned new skills along the way through his interactions with the outreach counselor and others. This included practicing coping strategies, identifying issues of rejection and loss, while better understanding its impact on his current relationships, enrolling in a culinary arts class to learn safe food handling and food preparation skills, participating in therapy and psychiatry, etc.

As Anthony came close to successfully completing his culinary arts class he was offered subsidized housing and support services via the Clubhouse's Next Step Program. This meant that his time at the shelter and his work with the outreach counselor were coming to a close. While the worker was excited to see Anthony prepare for graduation and housing placement, this resonated with Anthony in a far more negative way. In his world, moving onward was akin to rejection… just another place along the way that did not work out. In fact, Anthony assumed that people were happy to see him leave, rather than genuinely wanting to celebrate his accomplishments. It should be noted that this is not an uncommon occurrence among those who have experienced significant trauma and loss throughout their lives. They have lost so much, and have been mistreated so often, that it may deeply wound their sense of self-worth and cause them to question their value to others.

The termination process is a new and final stage to the counseling relationship, which exists on the knife's edge. It can become a vehicle for healing, or further loss and pain. Fortunately, the outreach counselor was successful at supporting transitions to a variety of services and resources, helping Anthony to develop new skills, as well as reviewing his accomplishments, and upholding his successes to the community through celebration. All of this was done while redefining their relationship from meeting several times a week for support, counseling and case management to being a supportive presence on standby, while others continued their work with Anthony. Of course, Anthony's journey will continue on without the outreach counselor's immediate presence, yet Anthony will always

> The termination process can become a vehicle for healing, or result in further loss and pain.

know that they shared a deep and successful connection. This was evidenced by their last interaction when Anthony shared, "I'll never forget all that you've done for me. I did my best to leave on a sour note and you wouldn't have it. I want to thank you for believing in me." The counselor adeptly responded, "Anthony, I'll never stop believing in you!" Something that had eluded Anthony for so many years now provides a foundation… perhaps the promise of greater success in future relationships, or at very least, knowing that it is possible.

References

Anthony, W., Cohen, M. & Farkas, M. (1990). *Psychiatric rehabilitation*. Boston University: Center for Psychiatric Rehabilitation.

Levy, J. S. (2013). *Pretreatment guide for homeless outreach & housing first: Helping couples, youth, and unaccompanied adults*. Ann Arbor, MI: Loving Healing Press.

Miller, W. R. & Rollnick, S. (1991). *Motivational interviewing: Preparing people to* change addictive behavior. New York: Guilford.

Prochaska, J. O. & DiClemente, C. C. (1982). Trans theoretical therapy: Toward a more integrative model of change. *Psychotherapy: Theory, Research, and Practice. 19(3): 276-288.*

Sartre, J. P. (1956). *Being and nothingness*. New York, New York: Washington Square Press.

Walter, J. & Peller, J. (1992). *Becoming solution-focused in brief therapy*. Chicago: Brunner/Mazel.

7 Supervision: Embracing PIE and Open Dialogue

Introduction

My last publication, *Cross-Cultural Dialogues on Homelessness* (Levy with Johnson, 2018), was a joint project that featured several authors from the UK. Through our collaboration, I learned about Psychologically Informed Environments (PIE), which is a relationship-centered approach that considers the impact of the physical and social environment on people, whether it be staff, clients, or a particular program or community (Johnson, 2013). PIE directs us to the importance of building community with the people we serve and has played a significant role in reshaping the culture of homeless hostels (aka. UK transitional housing settings) to be more inclusive and therapeutic. We can use PIE to support our staff members by establishing positive professional relationships that include all team members, as well as a culture of inquiry and reflective practice. Here, we apply psychological model(s) to guide supervisors and staff through the process of building a learning community that is empowered to help others. In this chapter, we apply the ecological lens of PIE and the psychological models of Pretreatment and Open Dialogue to staff supervision and facilitating collaborative working relationships across systems of care to better serve people who have experienced the effects of homelessness, trauma and loss. PIE, Pretreatment and Open Dialogue perspectives can be integrated into the supervision process on four different levels:

- Development of PIE Workplace
- Worker-Supervisor Relationship
- Client-Worker Relationship
- Worker-Systems Communication

The rest of this chapter will explore each of the above with a primary focus on developing a positive social environment and reflective practice for all staff members.

Development of PIE Workplace

Our challenge of providing support and supervision for our staff naturally mirrors the same challenges as working with our clients. This is due to the simple truth that people are people. Regardless of the who, it's all about getting person centered, fostering connections, giving voice, and establishing a sense of trust and autonomy. We are attempting to build a community where all are welcomed and heard… a real sense of inclusion!

Throughout this text, we have reviewed the value of Pretreatment as a psychological model for helping folks to build pathways to housing and recovery, which includes fostering meaningful connections with others. Here, I will present a compelling case that a Pretreatment perspective can pay dividends with staff supervision, satisfaction, and retention. However, first let's familiarize ourselves with an Open Dialogue approach and how it can be utilized in conjunction with Pretreatment to provide an inclusive and fertile environment for staff learning and practice. Or, as my colleagues from the UK would say, constructing a Psychologically Informed Environment (PIE) with staff.

Open Dialogue was developed and researched in Western Lapland (Finland) during the 1980s. It is a non-hierarchical approach to promoting recovery that facilitates positive communication and person-centered work with a focus on helping clients reconnect with and develop networks of social support. The clients, families, friends, social workers, psychiatrists and others are all on equal footing when it comes to discussions of what works, or what doesn't work for advancing the recovery process. Seikkula and others (2006, 2011) have studied effective approaches for people with schizophrenia, and have found that the Open Dialogue model focused on building and maintaining psychosocial support networks greatly reduced or in many instances eliminated the need for psychotropic medication as part of the recovery process. Open Dialogue does not follow a single top-down paradigm to treatment to guide the recovery process, so traditional psychiatric interventions may work for some, while a variety of different approaches (i.e., Peer Interventions, Recovery Coach and Programs, Self Help Groups, adding meaningful structure or activities, etc.) may be considered, and in fact may be a better fit, for others. The philosophical roots of Open Dialogue can be traced back to Mikhail Bakhtin's work on the philosophy of language (1981). The clear focus of this model is on facilitating a positive non-hierarchical welcomed communication, building client centered support networks and identifying their strengths, healthy activities, and community connections (natural supports) to foster recovery, growth, and wellbeing.

Psychological models of Pretreatment and Open Dialogue can be applied so that our staff of diverse cultural backgrounds, ethnicities, race, and of multidisciplinary fields of practice are comfortable bringing their individuality and expertise to the table. We are crossing cultural divides in an effort to engage in a productive dialogue that is supportive, instructive and empowering for all team members. Open Dialogue brings a non-hierarchical approach to the forefront by reframing all that we do with staff as co-vision, as opposed to supervision or putting one type of discipline or expertise above another. All are welcomed to give voice, and this is facilitated by the supervisors taking on the challenge to be person-centered with their team or individual workers, rather than simply managing programs. A process unfolds from simply managing, to providing supervision, which eventually transforms into co-vision.

In order to build a sense of team or community within any given program, it is helpful to provide the time and the space for that to happen. We must take the time to model and amplify supportive and appreciative staff behaviors by providing positive feedback through person-centered supervision. In essence, we are building trusting relationships that respect our workers' autonomy, while demarcating the time and space in our schedules to foster a sense of team, reflective practice and a culture of inquiry. For instance, the Homelessness Services program where I work provides many opportunities for teamwork development and reflective practice. This is done through monthly staff meetings, monthly Peer-Team group supervision, and at least twice per month individual co-vision sessions, as well as doing outreach in pairs and taking the time to debrief after outreach counseling meetings with clients. During the recent COVID pandemic, we opted for more outdoor meetings and multiple picnics, as well as other fun events to replace indoor staff meetings. Fortunately, staff are now vaccinated, so we have greater flexibility in regard to when and where we meet. Nevertheless, since the outdoor meetings and picnics were so engaging and had such a positive impact on our sense of team, we have decided to continue the practice indefinitely.

One of the central tasks of supervision is to support transitions. Whether it is the hiring or the orientation of a new employee, or when someone is leaving their job, the supervisor plays a critical role toward facilitating transformative moments of their professional practice. The heart of outreach counseling is relationship based, so proper orientation and termination will directly impact both the team and the clients we serve. The more we build a culture of teamwork and support, the more effective it is to involve other team members in the hiring and training of new staff, providing coverage during vacations, or transitioning as a worker is terminating employment. Before a new team member is added, our current staff interviews and gives feedback on all of the candidates for hire. We take the time to debrief after our group interviews in order to review the strengths/weaknesses and unique skills the candidates offer, such as being bilingual or having a background in creative expression therapies. In many cases we are drawn to intangible attributes such as the person's passion and sense of meaning in homelessness work, overall team fit, or having an engaging presence, as well as more concrete considerations such as the importance of adding diversity to our team in regard to race, ethnicity, gender, culture (inclusive of LGBTQ identity) and age, or having their own firsthand experience of homelessness and recovery. Throughout my career as a manager and supervisor, I have learned the wisdom of trusting the group to make the best decision for building our staff community, and thereby giving everyone a sense of ownership in the process of team building, training, and orientation.

A new employee joining our team is oriented through one-on-one and group supervision, provided with literature on homelessness, a listing of area services and resources, as well as given an array of policies and procedures to help organize their work. My organization even goes as far as to provide a week of extensive training inclusive of reviewing privacy, confidentiality and mandated reporting standards, corporate compliance procedures and a review of potential boundary violations and vital counseling skills such as Suicide Assessment and Motivational Interviewing techniques, as well as

CPR/First Aid Certification. I like to send new workers on three separate outreach missions where they shadow highly skilled veteran employees. Immediately afterward, we meet to debrief and review whatever reflections and questions they may have. This process simultaneously trains a new worker, strengthens the team, and sets the table for effective ongoing supervision/co-vision.

Nationally, there has been a federal initiative to integrate Peers with our PATH (Projects Assisting Transitions from Homelessness) Outreach Teams[7]. I have managed several PATH Outreach Teams across Massachusetts and have had the pleasure of hiring, supervising and overseeing the integration of Peer Specialists with existing clinically trained team members. This is not as distinct as it sounds, as I have always been in favor of hiring team members who are both clinically trained and have developed expertise through firsthand experience. This has resulted in many staff members utilizing their personal recovery from mental health concerns, addiction, and/or homelessness to inform their day-to-day work. It also means that self-care and establishing a culture with staff that values their health is critical to our success and wellbeing. My experience of working with Peer Specialists has demonstrated the importance of checking in on their own recovery work and stability, as well as managing boundaries with the clients they serve. The challenges of working in homelessness environments with people who have experienced trauma similar to your own personal experiences can trigger past traumatic events that may compromise one's judgment due to a fight/flight/freeze response. All of this only differs from our supervisory work with all of our staff members in the degree of the support needed and the careful development of a distinct Peer Specialist role, while the core issues of helping our staff to stay emotionally centered and mange triggers for everyone remains virtually the same.

Whether it is Peer or non-peer staff, staying emotionally centered and healthy is a key component to providing quality outreach services, and therefore must be formally addressed by providing opportunities for reflective practice, and adequate support and supervision of staff. Our challenge as a diverse team with multiple personal experiences, differing levels of education and different areas of expertise has been to find a common language to inform our mission of outreach and engagement with people experiencing homelessness. In essence, we are hoping to balance general training protocols with effective individualization of the supervisory process to better meet the needs and strengths of our workers. Coming together around our joint mission in support of one another is an empowering experience. A Pretreatment approach as a guide for informing staff supervision, client assessment and enhancing communication between staff members through a common language has served this purpose.

Importantly, we know that homelessness service workers bear witness to trauma and loss as a normal part of their workday. We therefore need to provide supportive forums for frontline staff to process potentially traumatic field experiences. Non-hierarchical Peer support groups and 1:1 co-vision sessions are particularly effective for promoting the self-care required for sustaining a sense of balance and connection, rather than feeling overwhelmed, isolated, and vicariously traumatized. The work we ask our staff to do is very demanding and emotionally draining. It takes a broad range of skills and adequate support to do it effectively. The development of a PIE Workplace for staff can make a positive difference

---

[7] The hiring of "experts from experience" to better inform programs and provide greater sensitivity and support to the clients that are served is also valued by PIE enthusiasts throughout the UK and elsewhere.

in the quality of the services delivered. Regularly scheduled Group and individual meetings with staff assure the opportunity to support one another by reflecting on cases, debriefing after difficult or challenging interactions with clients or workers from other programs, as well as an opportunity to process loss and genuinely connect with fellow human service travelers who are on the same journey. Our facilitation of strong supportive connections among staff members, developing a greater sense of team and belongingness to something larger than ourselves, as well as finding and embracing meaning throughout our work are keys to the PIE workplace and our ongoing success in the field.

Exercise 7-1: Finding a Sense of Meaning in the Workplace

What is most meaningful about your work?

_____

_____

_____

_____

_____

Here's a helpful hint: This may include connecting to something larger than yourself or you may want to reflect on how your individuality is creatively expressed through your work with others (staff and clients), or valuable life lessons you have learned.

Discussion

The PIE workplace experience can be enhanced by helping staff to reconnect to the personal meaning of their work. One example, among many, is that we have incorporated a new staff welcoming ritual, which transforms our staff meeting into a celebration for the new worker. This is done by breaking bread together (e.g., Coffee and Danish), partaking in an open dialogue about our PATH mission and the successes or accomplishments of our team, as well as asking each staff member to check-in and reflect upon what they find meaningful in their work. Upon the end of our group reflection, the new worker gets to express to the group whatever comes to mind. Each time we do this, staff members report feeling reinvigorated and proud of the work they do, while the new worker feels thoroughly welcomed and part of the fold. It is a powerful experience that reflects a belonging to something larger than just our individual experiences... a real sense of team and mission!

I have found a great deal of meaning in my own journey of working with people who have experienced homelessness. I have witnessed firsthand the strength of the human spirit regardless of the harsh environments and negative messages people without homes are forced to endure. I have learned the valuable lesson of appreciation. I no longer take for granted my own mental and physical health, connections with family and friends, the warmth of being indoors, or the comfort of sleeping in a bed. I have become closer with my fellow staff members and have gotten great value from hearing their stories and providing a calm space for reflective practice. The next section further reflects on "meaning making" and connecting to staff's strengths, values, and personal stories within the context of their work with clients.

Worker-Supervisor Relationship

Our main objective as supervisors is to form a trusting and supportive relationship with staff members, while upholding and facilitating the application of their various strengths and aptitudes to their work. Over the years of doing supervision, I have found that the most successful employees were unique individuals who found meaning in their vocation. They have such a strong sense of mission that helping the homeless becomes an essential part of their identity. It is important to help facilitate the *meaning making* process for staff, and to respect their individuality by giving voice to their stories. This encompasses the telling of their own work narratives, as well as hearing other team members tell the many client stories they have encountered over the weeks and months of outreach.

In many ways, the challenges of working with staff mirror our work with clients. On the one hand, the five principles of Pretreatment can serve as a guide toward developing positive and productive dialogue with staff in regard to their particular strengths and sense of meaning. On the other, our goal is to successfully pass on the basic principles and underpinnings of a Pretreatment philosophy to staff, so that they can apply it directly to their work with clients. In essence we are helping our staff to utilize their narrative and unique skills within the shared context of a Pretreatment framework. This helps staff move beyond the reliance on solely the "art" of relationship building, scaffolding a more professional and proven approach to the work. This approach is effective at harnessing staff's passion and creativity, while staying true to the central task of better serving their clients through a person-centered approach.

It is critical that workers are provided with an appropriate venue and guidance to tell their stories. They've gone on countless journeys with the clients they are trying to help, and have a great deal to share with one another. Whether it is success stories, specific dilemmas, or traumatic experiences, much can be learned. Through this kind of sharing and feedback, outreach counselors can begin to balance their limitations with what is possible, and thereby achieve the sense of serenity and perspective required to continually do this work well. A culture of sharing and providing each other with support needs to be initially facilitated and reinforced by the supervisor. This includes establishing a group process where outreach workers become comfortable presenting cases, sharing grief and loss issues, as well as seeking support and consultation from team members. If we are to be successful in maintaining highly qualified staff long-term, then we need to provide the opportunities for high quality 1:1 co-vision and peer group support. This is essential because the effectiveness of a Pretreatment approach is ultimately dependent upon staff being nimble, sensitive and responsive to a broad range of issues and challenges that will inevitably come up with clients and service providers.

Dr. Ray Middleton (Levy with Johnson, 2013, p. xiii) states, "I have found that taking an Open Dialogue approach does help staff reduce their anxiety through accepting they only ever partly know what is going on with clients. It also helps staff appreciate that we understand the client's world dialogically from the *relatively remote context* of our own narrative world."

The Open Dialogue approach applies directly to our co-vision with staff, and impacts its delivery and tone. The co-vision process is based on inquiry, exploration, and learning together, rather than putting pressure on any given person to simply know. While none of us have all the answers, we can journey and learn together about what might work best for our clients in any given moment or particular circumstance, as well as to understand what hasn't worked, or what has been detrimental. Upon asking this critical question, we can then apply the principles of Pretreatment to guide our reflective practice. This leads to a deeper understanding of what interventions are effective versus what is leading to greater difficulty within the worker-client relationship. Is it connected to the worker-client stage of engagement, or perhaps needing to develop the playground of language to a greater extent, so the client is not triggered by the words and ideas we present? As we offer assistance, are we aware of the transition processes the client is currently experiencing? If working on particular goals or challenges with the client, have we properly aligned our interventions with the corresponding stage of change? Have we done a safety assessment to consider whether or not we take the more active and directive stance a crisis demands versus a more passive, yet supportive, harm reduction approach?

Potential, and perhaps very initial, pretreatment pathways for helping ourselves, our team and clients arise in the midst of reflective practice, and within the context of our supervisor-worker relationship and the ever-evolving common language. That being said… so much depends on how things unfold in the day-to-day work in the field between clients and workers, so let's examine that more closely in the next section. Ultimately, it is the people without homes who are our teachers, or as it is commonly stated in narrative circles (Epston and White, 1992), "People are experts on their own worlds."

Client-Worker Relationship

A supervisor with an understanding of a Pretreatment paradigm and its applications of the five principles of care can be an effective guide for workers and clients in pursuit of person-centered, goal driven work. Outreach counselors, clinicians, case managers and Housing First staff, among others, working with populations that are often untreated and pre-contemplative can benefit from the opportunity for regular case review and feedback. When faced with chronic and acute issues, it is easy for staff to feel frustrated and to lose hope. The supervisor needs to provide an experienced perspective and facilitate a sense of optimism and equilibrium. This requires sharing challenging cases, situations, and successes from the past. By utilizing Pretreatment principles mixed with past and present case narratives, we can help staff to discover productive pathways for helping.

When working with people who experience long-term homelessness, addressing their safety and immediacy needs is often the doorway for promoting the change process. Ultimately it is the supervisor's job to provide guidance, boost morale and instill hope. I can recall several occasions when direct care staff were beginning to give up on aiding hard-to-engage clients. In response, we explored the application of different Pretreatment strategies and then proceeded to discuss potential pathways for helping. This process is exemplified in Chapter 4 and Judy's story. Here, the supervisor provides the outreach counselor with the reflective practice space to explore how to best engage with a very guarded and often angry potential client. As the outreach counselor shared Judy's narrative with his supervisor, it became evident that Judy valued "safety" and this was reflected in part by keeping her belongings secure from people, chipmunks and other rodents. Together, we (through the co-vision process) devised an offering of addressing Judy's immediate needs through a housing and safe storage plan. We chose precise wording and discussed the timing of our offer with the hope that it could more readily resonate in her world. Throughout these types of joint efforts, I encourage staff to contemplate constructing a common language with their clients, so we can better understand the person's world, rather than blindly making offerings of services and resources. Or, as Dr. Ray Middleton (Levy with Johnson, 2018, p. xiii) states, "Drawing on Bakhtin's concepts, I encourage staff to see both themselves and their clients temporarily journeying together, meeting dialogically in overlapping worlds as unfinalised personalities, who can listen to and learn from each other at crossroads on our life-journeys." Through strong engagement and Open Dialogue with our clients, we can jointly explore, discover or even create possible Pretreatment pathways toward healing.

Outreach and engagement practices with chronically homeless persons are purposely informal in nature. This can lead to difficulties in attaining and maintaining appropriate boundaries with clients. This is one of the core challenges throughout the stages of outreach and engagement. Supervision can be used to reflect on thorny issues such as when does it make sense to feed dependency needs, as well as providing a more in-depth consideration of how to form and reinforce boundaries in various homeless venues. The formation of boundaries based on the outreach-counseling developmental model (refer back to Table 2 – p. 15) and the five principles of Pretreatment, was first presented in the book *Homeless Narratives & Pretreatment Pathways* (2010) and is reprised here for your consideration.

Clearly, the Engagement process begins informally, and dependency needs are fed during the Pre-engagement stage in order to foster initial communication. During this phase, we may offer need items to clients and communication begins more on the clients' terms, as we seek permission to enter and understand their world. We are challenged by the process of developing boundaries because we don't have a clear set of office-based rules and duties (Office Culture) to guide us. As communication becomes more welcome, we enter the Engagement stage. This is when we begin to define boundaries more firmly by introducing and reviewing our roles as outreach counselors and what duties that can potentially entail. During the Engagement stage, we foster a common language with the aim of defining mutually acceptable goals that can guide our work into the Contracting stage. Upon contracting with clients our roles and duties are further defined, clarified, and reinforced. During the Contract Implementation phase, we provide a counseling relationship that supports client ownership of goals and initiative for positive change. During this phase, supporting transitions to housing and/or treatment related services (i.e., day programs, Community Health and MH clinics, addiction programs, etc.) are critical. We may need to temporarily increase our level of support to promote the bridging process and adaptation to these new environments, people, and ideas. Upon entering the stage of Termination, it is best if our roles and boundaries are redefined in conjunction with the client's progress of engaging and contracting with other providers.

Over time, the outreach-counseling relationship comes to an end. However, if the client were to re-experience homelessness, we may provide short-term intervention and redirection to housing and support services. Both the client and counselor experience issues of loss, which can result in the counselor and client over-reaching newly defined boundaries (role confusion). An additional consideration is that crisis can occur during any phase of the outreach-counseling process. An individual in crisis is having difficulty with adaptive functioning in critical areas necessary for self-care, and is struggling with acute issues. Crisis intervention dictates that the counselor takes a more directive stance, inclusive of feeding dependency, to assure safety. Finally, a Harm Reduction model can further guide our work. Need items such as clothes, food, blankets, and even clean needles may be offered at different stages of the counseling process, and apart from crisis situations, to help assure future safety, and/or reduce the risk of harm to self or others. Arguably, this may also feed dependency rather than self-sufficiency, but it is at times necessary to promote safety via both harm reduction and crisis intervention strategies. The stages of the developmental counseling process rarely proceed in such a linear fashion. This is important to note when reviewing any type of Stage Theory (i.e., Stages of engagement, Phases of common Language, or Change Model, etc.). At any point, a client may revert back to a previous stage and it is up to the worker to remain aligned with stage-appropriate interventions.

Outreach work to under-served populations can and does elicit powerful feelings and behaviors from the counselor such as wanting to save or take care of clients, frustrations with perceived lack of progress, trying to dictate or control outcomes, and becoming overly authoritative or angry with other providers, etc. It is important that the worker has the opportunity to voice and reflect upon these feelings and behaviors; otherwise, the counselor's judgment and interventions may be compromised or become ineffective. Particular phases of relationship formation are apt to elicit these types of responses. During the Pre-engagement phase, the worker often struggles with the impulse to "save" the client from danger, or his or her own fears of the homeless world. The impulse to "save" may cause the worker to be overly aggressive and thereby take unwarranted safety risks, or push the work too quickly without attention to the client's need for an incremental transition. An overly fearful tendency may cause the worker to proceed too cautiously, thereby missing opportunities to engage with clients. The goal of Pre-engagement is to establish a sense of safety via an initial welcomed communication, which will hopefully lead to further engagement.

Throughout the phase of Engagement, the worker may struggle with feelings of wanting to take care of the client, or with the belief that a homeless person must take responsibility for his or her own situation. If either tendency is taken to an extreme, it will interfere with both boundary definition and role development between worker and client. The challenge of the engagement phase is to establish an ongoing communication that promotes trust and respects autonomy, while further defining roles and boundaries. Similarly, throughout the stage of Contracting, the worker may struggle with being too directive or fostering complete client autonomy without providing adequate guidance. Either of these tendencies, taken to an extreme, can reinforce a homeless person's sense of shame and guilt, rather than promote independence. The challenge is to facilitate the client's exploration of possible goals and interests, so that he or she can experience a sense of autonomy and initiative throughout the process of contract development. This type of analysis can also be done regarding an array of relationship-based issues that arise throughout the outreach-counseling process, including but not limited to issues of shame, guilt, anger, grief and loss. Supervision, whether it be peer supervision or with a clinical supervisor, provides the sense of grounding and centering needed to help workers stay on task.

Common pitfalls can be mitigated by understanding that assessment is truly a fluid and dynamic process. Interventions that may be an important harm reduction strategy at one phase of the engagement or change process may be enabling during a different phase. This is part of exposing the myth that the worker should never work harder than the client. The reality is that in order to be successful with Housing First, outreach, and a Pretreatment approach, we will sometimes be required to work much harder than the client. This is particularly true during the early stages of engagement, as well as during crisis and transition points with people who are refusing treatment, yet experience major mental illnesses and addictions. At the same time, we need to be savvy in our interventions, so they are congruent with the particular stage of engagement, common language construction, and change that is most relevant to the client's circumstances. Supervision can help workers to focus on the application of these different stage-based models in order to more effectively "get where the client is at." The nature of these stage-based models, whether it be in regard to phases of change, engagement, or common language development, is that they provide a roadmap and with it direction and hope for improvement.

Worker-Systems Communication

Michael Rowe (1999, p. 1) states, "Homeless encounters take place at a border that divides one world from another." It is up to the outreach counselor to be adept at getting to know both the world of the potential client and the array of available resources and services. Through the process of engagement and common language development we are able to understand the words, ideas, values, culture, challenges, needs, wants, goals, and aspirations that make up the client's world. If we are to be effective at introducing or matching our clients to available resources and services, then we will also need to work with other systems of care and thereby gain an understanding of the culture of these systems, their eligibility criteria, target populations served, and the nature of services and resources offered. This means getting to know the contact people associated with these resources and services, and the many different houses of language each of these individual programs employ. The success of our referrals resulting in client placement is often directly influenced by both our understanding of who is a good match to what program, as well as the quality of our relationship with the contact people who govern eligibility, intake, and transition to their programs.

The culture and language spoken can vary greatly from the clinical worlds of addiction or mental health programs to faith-based social services, or social justice advocacy that upholds the human rights of oppressed groups and individuals. In other words, on both the systems and individual levels, the challenge to care is to foster collaborative professional relationships based on a common language and purpose. A productive and open dialogue that crosses cultural divides can lead to successful matches between these often disparate worlds of the individuals in need and available resources and services. It is not an overstatement to say that the success of our work hinges on our ability to be interpreters and bridge-builders.

Our role as supervisors and program managers is to build Pretreatment pathways to the many houses of language that make up our service and resource networks, and in turn better help our staff to successfully navigate these options. Outreach services are provided in a range of settings from directly on the streets and in the woods to the shelters and various peer networks (e.g., recovery centers) and/or other resource settings (e.g. meal programs) that folks visit. So, conflicts, adversarial stances, or just lack of collaboration between our staff and the folks who manage these community programs and services may not only restrict client access via our referral, but also our direct access to the very people we are hoping to identify and serve.

Example 7-1: The Quest for Productive Dialogue

I am reminded of a recent example of a conflict from within our Continuum of Care (CoC) which not only led to high levels of frustration, anger and lack of collaboration among providers, but also temporarily resulted in poor delivery of resources and services to some highly vulnerable persons. This occurred during 2020 in conjunction with the change of season from autumn to winter. A number of experts from experience who provide volunteer outreach and peer services in a small Western MA town focused their social justice efforts on homelessness. They gave voice for an array of folks who continued to sleep rough including those in the woods, hallways, abandoned buildings and vehicles, as well as for others who were temporarily but not stably housed, living in motels, doubled up with friends, or couch surfing. The advocates also pointed out that they thought the local homelessness shelter provider was not properly doing the work of helping those who were most in need. This was cause for even greater concern than normal as we were in the midst of the COVID pandemic. The advocates reported high numbers of vulnerable people in urgent need of safe accommodation to the local Continuum of Care (CoC), Town and statewide officials, and virtually anyone else who might listen, including the local press. Soon thereafter, with service providers and advocates working from different houses of language, some troubling conflicts arose.

Most notably, lots of finger pointing followed as service providers and advocates took on a defensive rather than a collaborative posture. Our Zoom meetings and phone calls to try and sort through these thorny issues became heated or avoidant by resorting to more of a silo mentality. In other words, it was far easier for CoC providers to state that many of the folks that the advocates declared as homeless and vulnerable were in fact not literally homeless or HUD eligible, or for advocates to state that the system and its providers of services were ineffective and non-caring. In addition, shelter staff provided some outreach at local parks and came across far fewer people than previously reported, so they felt comfortable stating that the numbers of unsheltered homeless were being exaggerated. Many assumptions were made on both sides without the benefit of productive and sustained dialogue.

Unfortunately, some folks remained outside throughout the entire winter, even though the local homeless shelter had at least ten openings on any given night. This was in part blamed on the lack of positive relationships and distrust between the advocates and shelter workers, which only further frayed their relations. However, there were other factors to consider, as many people sleeping rough had experienced significant trauma and therefore did not feel safe in highly stimulating shelter environments. Or, some refused to give up their sense of freedom and access to drugs and alcohol, in exchange for a shelter bed with specific rules and expectations. Still others sleeping rough claimed to have negative past experiences at the shelter and would not return under any circumstances. Meanwhile, some surrounding towns in Western MA, with a more collaborative approach, more readily expanded access for people sleeping rough through motel dollars from the Department of Housing and Community Development, resulting in a network of shelters and motels with semi-private rooms helping to drastically reduce the sleeping rough population.

During our first couple of co-vision sessions, our local outreach counselor described the situation as quite charged with many different organizations and people being in conflict with one another. At first, we decided to steer clear of the conflict and lie low while continuing to do our direct work with people experiencing homelessness. We elected this strategy based on wanting to stay on good terms and well-engaged with everyone including shelter staff and advocates, while hoping that things would slowly work their way out. However, the issue not only persisted, but escalated with the local press interviewing advocates, and fielding complaints from some people who were sleeping rough without a safe place to reside during a pandemic and cold New England winter.

Approximately one month prior to the newspaper coverage, the worker and I changed our stance with both providers and advocates, from being a more passive harm reduction approach to active crisis intervention. In other words, we decided to lean in and embrace the crisis/opportunity at hand, rather than to watch things slowly but surely unravel. This is harder than it seems, since our initial stance was protective and more in line with our emotions to turn away from the difficulties that a crisis often brings. In fact, the only way for this to happen was by our co-vision dialogue or reflective practice being focused on our mission, while encouraging an open dialogue on what was working vs. what wasn't working on the community and systems levels. We soon realized the moral imperative or obligation to change our stance, if we were to remain on the mission of reaching out and assisting the most vulnerable among us. The worker and I collaborated on the process of bringing adversarial players on to the same playground of language.

Since none of the other area human service providers appeared to be engaging well with the advocates, we reached out to engage them in dialogue. Our goal, as it would be with any other service provider, was to better understand their words, ideas, and values with an aim of collaborating to better serve our clients and the community. So, we identified the lead advocate-volunteer who was providing outreach services, as well as the director for the local peer-led recovery center. We had also already established the beginnings of a working relationship with one of their peer staff members, so our outreach counselor reached out to him as well. These efforts were focused on building trust with our contacts and inviting them to participate on a range of issues such as contributing to the yearly HUD

Point in Time unsheltered homeless count to actively encouraging them to refer people who were sleeping rough to us for further assessment, services, motel stay, and housing referral.

The co-vision sessions between the outreach counselor and me now concentrated on the steps to enhance engagement with peer workers and volunteer advocates. Simultaneously, we explained to the other providers and the local lead agency for the CoC that we were focused on *our mission,* and so our engagement with everyone who works with a homeless population is an essential part of the process. This also meant that we were changing the whole tenor of the communication from hierarchical and judgmental to more of an open dialogue. As we had learned to do so well with our clients, we were now willing to take the risk of not knowing what exact challenges an Open Dialogue would bring, while believing in the unfolding process of building positive relationships based on a common language and delineating reachable goals.

As the lead outreach volunteer advocate connected more with our local CoC, she gained a better understanding of the array of services being offered by different HUD funded agencies inclusive of homelessness prevention, rapid re-housing, homeless outreach, and permanent supportive housing. This led to a joint assessment of the different sub-populations the advocates and volunteers were serving, and some positive movement toward ferreting out who qualified for what types of assistance. In essence, we developed a common language based on these categories, eligibility criteria, in conjunction with the advocates informing us about the surprisingly large numbers of people who remained under-served and highly vulnerable. In time, my communications with the lead outreach advocate and some of the folks via the peer run recovery center served as a bridge for them to better understand eligibility to different programs and better ways to proceed with referrals. This reduced conflict with other providers, including shelter staff and us, and improved access to services for some of their participants. In turn, this helped my local outreach counselor to be alerted to a wider group of folks who clearly could benefit from his services, and the local CoC coordinator developed a greater awareness of on-the-ground concerns of vulnerable subgroups. Finally, the table was now set for a more productive dialogue that questioned entrenched local and statewide policies in regard to homeless prevention practices and shelter versus motel access for those sleeping rough.

Questions for Consideration

Q1 In the previous example, how many different "Houses of Language" can you identify? Describe each "House of Language."

Here's a helpful hint: Every group identified throughout the example represents a "House of Language." What are their ideas, values, mission?

Q2: Compare the different "Houses of Language." How are they in line with or in conflict with one another?

Here's a helpful hint: Think about the mission, values, and functions associated with each house.

Reflections and Possibilities

As it turned out, the social justice house of language widely practiced by the peer network and others defined homelessness in a different and broader manner than HUD's literal homelessness definition, so it was at times in conflict with the shelter providers' house of language and limited role in the Continuum of Care (CoC). The HUD house of language also included the different types of services and eligibility criteria practiced by local service providers inclusive of homelessness prevention, rapid re-housing, homeless outreach, and permanent supportive housing. My consultation provided translation and mediation with the lead outreach volunteer and other peer workers with the hope of improving communication with local homelessness service providers and the lead CoC agency. Understandably, the volunteers, peer workers, and advocates were joined in wanting much more for an under-served population, which ranged from people sleeping rough to those who were impoverished and unstably housed. It should be noted that these under-served sub-populations also reside in their own houses of language and the client narratives discussed throughout this book provide detail examples.

It should be noted that the PATH outreach counselor and I were both trained in psychology, and so were primarily housed in a clinical language, though we continued to expand our frontiers in an attempt to communicate well with multiple systems of care and all of the agencies, programs, services, and resources that followed. We aspired to be interpreters and bridge builders in an effort to better serve those in need.

Systems advocacy and collaborative relationships among providers, concerned community members, and under-served subgroups can be enhanced through the use of Pretreatment and Open Dialogue.

> We reap multiple benefits by looking through the many and varied lenses of the different houses of language.

Today, this remains an unfolding process with all of the challenges, conflicts, and difficulties one might expect, though at least we have moved toward improved communication with a greater sense of common purpose to provide greater access to motel beds and affordable housing options with support services. Our hope is to lean into identifying the barriers to care and what is needed to be successful in our mission to end homelessness. There is so much to be gained by looking through the many and varied lenses of the different houses of language. Over the many years of listening to people's stories, bearing witness to their struggles, strengths and aspirations, I have come to believe that as long as we embrace inclusion rather than division, diversity is our most valuable resource. This is true when it comes to the people we serve, as it is for the many providers of services.

Four Levels of Supervision and Data Collection

In this chapter, we reviewed the four levels of the supervision process as follows:

- PIE Workplace

- Worker-Supervisor Relationship

- Client-Worker Relationship

- Worker-Systems Communication

We began with the PIE Workplace in order to set the proper environment and culture for establishing an open dialogue that promotes an inclusive community for staff. We worked to strengthen the worker-supervisor relationship, and transform the supervision process into one that is centered on the empowerment of staff and co-vision, as opposed to being overly managed with top-down dictates. This was by putting relationships, at all levels, at the center of our work when utilizing Pretreatment principles and Open Dialogue. Similarly, we encouraged the exploration of the client-worker relationship by jointly utilizing a Pretreatment assessment to guide us in the development of person-centered work. Finally, we reviewed the importance of fostering collaborative relationships throughout many programs and systems of care in order to support client transitions and more effectively advocate for greater access to needed resources and services.

The question that remains is how to best evaluate or measure the progress of our work. Promoting a psychologically informed workplace for our staff is central, so we certainly don't want to bludgeon our staff with data requirements, yet we do need effective quantitative and qualitative measures. Collecting data serves us well if it enhances our work and measures our progress, while also pointing out challenges, or areas in need of growth, as opposed to undermining the central process of person-centered work between clients and staff, and/or staff members and their supervisors.

Over the past few years, I have been approached by many program managers struggling with the difficulty of the ever-increasing demand for data and its negative impact on staff morale and productivity. Increasing data demands result in staff being less in the field and doing more office work to keep up, or may compromise the relationship-building process due to staff asking more pointed and intrusive questions early on in the engagement process with clients. In search of more data points, we have inadvertently imposed extensive intake processes that are at best disengaging, and at worse re-traumatizing clients.

In response to this dilemma, I have proposed a two-tier process to sort out data collection demands. This addresses the question of how our work with new or prospective clients can uphold the engagement process, while collecting initial critical data. What do we truly need to know from our initial contacts with prospective clients? Designing a data system to fit a model of outreach and engagement upholds the value of developing a trusting relationship above all else. A two-tier model has the ability to initially open a client without full enrollment. This initial or first tier of opening simply counts contact sessions and provides some measure based on the stages of engagement without the need for formal documentation such as intakes, various assessments, and service plans, which are done only after being fully enrolled (second tier of data system). Based on the stages of engagement, the contacts with potential clients may be officially tracked by contact notes, but not yet fully enrolled in our data system as follows:

- First Stage of Engagement Process (aka: pre-engagement): The goal is to establish a welcomed initial communication, which includes providing need items, basic safety assessment, and desensitizing the client to the worker's presence via introductions by others or modeling our work by providing outreach to others in general vicinity of client, etc.

- Second Stage of Engagement Process (aka: engagement): The goal is to establish welcomed ongoing communication, which includes defining roles/boundaries and understanding client wants/needs and language, etc.

- Third Stage of Engagement Process (aka: contracting): The objective is to translate the client's needs/wants, values and aspirations into workable goals that are in line with our job role as defined by our program. *Once this is attained, the client is then enrolled and officially enters the second tier of the data system, which requires more documentation.*

Where I currently work, we have the ability to open cases and do contact notes without enrollment and thereby eliminate the need to meet the full range of data requirements from the outset. Once the third stage of the Engagement process (aka: contracting) is reached, then we consider enrollment into our program. Enrollment into a given program of services requires additional data points via an intake and other assessments. As we become goal focused in our work, the initial contact notes that simply focused on safety issues and the stage of the Engagement process for unenrolled clients are now transformed into progress notes for those enrolled, based on the client's needs/wants and goals (tracking progress). The reality is that we regularly engage with people, enroll them into our programs or services, and then sometimes find that we are unable to continue the work for a variety of reasons. By taking a two-tiered approach, we can initially save staff time, while assuring that the push for data is not one of the reasons for disenrollment.

Typical data measures of the effectiveness of the client-worker relationship are both qualitative and quantitative. This includes client satisfaction surveys, tracking referrals made and successful placements into housing and other resources and services (i.e., treatment for addiction, medical, and mental health issues, peer programs, benefits, etc.), as well as number of contacts with potential clients and program enrollments. If we are to look at this through the lens of empowering our staff and enhancing their work, then we ought to design these measures by inviting their input. What would be helpful for them? This is in line with promoting both worker-supervisor relationships, as well as the PIE Workplace culture. In essence, we are once again practicing the art of engagement and common language construction between all parties (direct care staff, data analysts, supervisors, and managers) in order to have an open and productive dialogue on the issue of data collection. The success of creating a very inclusive and empowering environment for our staff to work in can also be measured in several ways: staff satisfaction surveys, job retention rates, exit interviews, and meaningful participation in the many offerings of reflective practice via staff meetings, Peer-Team Supervision, 1:1 co-vision, and attendance at other gatherings such as team picnics or guest training opportunities, etc.

Finally, it is important to make note of a program's standing within the provider community. As mentioned earlier, our efforts are to remain in positive standing with all of the essential resource and service providers that interface regularly with our potential and current clients. This can also be measured by asking program providers to fill out satisfaction surveys about our services, as well as by tracking successful client referrals and placements, and gauging the degree and frequency of ongoing and unresolved conflicts resulting in formally filed complaints. Another potential indicator is how quickly the word spreads in regard to job openings at your organization, and the number of applications received for available positions. Ending where I started, I am compelled to reiterate that data collection should not become the main driver of the supervision process. Rather, it should be part of all four levels of supervision in a relationship centered approach. Putting data collection at the forefront of supervision is a mistake that has caused many services and programs to create an uncomfortable environment for staff. This ultimately leads to compromised relationships and poor outcomes regardless of how statistics may appear to show successful outcomes.

Through our simultaneous work on all four levels of supervision, we are able to develop a learning community that values person-centered, relationship-driven reflective practice, and a culture of inquiry for all its members. Here, the principles of Pretreatment, PIE, and Open Dialogue are integrated in an effort to better inform the supervision process inclusive of data collection. In combination, we can attain an important flow to our work; a sense of unity and belongingness to a mission that drives us to provide quality and targeted services that reach out to the most vulnerable among us.

References

Bakhtin, M. M. (1981). *The Dialogical Imagination*. Austin, TX: University of Texas Press.

Epston, D. & White, M. (1992). *Experience, contradiction, narrative, and imagination: Selected papers of David Epston and Michael White, 1989-1991*. Adelaide, Australia: Dulwich Centre Publications.

Johnson, R. (2013) Editorial: The concept of a "Psychologically Informed Environment" in *Housing Care and Support,* 15(2): Retrieved from:
http://www.emeraldinsight.com/products/journals/journals.htm?id=hcs

Levy, J. S. (2010). *Homeless narratives & pretreatment pathways: From words to housing*. Ann Arbor, MI: Loving Healing Press.

Levy, J. S. with Johnson, R. (2018). *Cross-cultural dialogues on homelessness: From* pretreatment strategies to psychological environments. Ann Arbor, MI: Loving Healing Press.

Rowe, M. (1999). *Crossing the Border*. Berkeley: University of California Press.

Seikkula, J. (2011). Becoming Dialogical: Psychotherapy or a way of Life? *The Australian and New Zealand Journal of Family Therapy*. 32(3): 179-193

Siekkula, J. & Arnkil, T. E. (2006). *Dialogical Meetings in Social Networks*. London, UK: Karnac (Books) Ltd.

8 Conclusion: People's Stories and Pretreatment Pathways to Better Health

"Loving-kindness is essentially a form of inclusiveness of caring, rather than categorizing others in terms of those whom we care for and those who can be easily excluded, ignored or disdained… A deepening of insight will inevitably include seeing how all of our lives are inextricably interconnected."

— Sharon Salzberg (2011)

Public Health Policy and Homelessness

As I write this final chapter, we are in the midst of a pandemic. Even though it has been and continues to be a difficult and stressful journey, my engagement with the work has taken on added meaning. The pandemic has brought to the forefront the inequities people without homes face on all levels. How is it that a civilized society has tolerated thousands upon thousands of people sleeping rough for so long? How do we tell people with a straight face that there is no room at the shelter, while offering no other safe alternatives? Or, conversely, how have we convinced ourselves that sheltering folks through the frigid nights of winter is a compassionate enough practice, as we close seasonal shelters at the beginning of each spring and thereby leave so many with no place to go? It is easy to question these habitual practices when your job is to provide outreach services to people sleeping rough. Through our outreach lens we see firsthand the unhealthy and at times deadly consequences of living in harsh and unsafe environments. Yet, through this public health crisis, our sense of normalcy has unraveled, bringing forth the opportunity to do things differently and with greater compassion.

Public Health policy has dictated that people sleeping rough should be offered extended motel/hotel stays to help stem the spread of the Pandemic, as opposed to letting people overcrowd our shelters. Policy makers finally had to face the fact that "business as usual" during COVID includes people without homes roaming about their cities and towns without access to indoor resources such as meal programs, cafes, libraries, or even bathrooms. Fortunately, the new policy of providing people sleeping rough quick access to motels/hotels with support services has gone into effect throughout Western MA, as well as throughout many, though not all, cities and towns across the US and UK. The change in policy has brought about a new dawn of multi-agency efforts to offer resources to our many unaffiliated hotel/motel guests, as well as to place folks as rapidly as possible into affordable housing units with support services. As a result, we have not only seen a low spread of COVID among a homeless and vulnerable population in Western MA, but we have also dramatically reduced the number of people sleeping rough. Let's hope that the lessons learned from this crisis result in long-term policy changes, which include viewing the issue of homelessness, and in particular people sleeping rough, through a public health lens that demands immediate action.

In fact, the Housing First movement has done just that, though it has not had the full support and investment of our government and the public health sector. There have been numerous studies (Roncarati, 2016; O'Connell, 2005; O'Connell & Swain, 2005) to demonstrate the health risks and costs of people sleeping rough inclusive of premature death and high-end utilization of emergency rooms and frequent hospitalizations. Research on Housing First (Bretherton & Pleace, 2015; Tsemberis, 2010; Stefancic & Tsemberis, 2007) has also shown how stable affordable housing with support services reduces healthcare costs and leads to improved health outcomes as evidenced by less emergency room usage and hospitalizations. These studies and many others have now firmly established the accepted truth held by homelessness advocates since the 1980s that proclaims affordable and stable housing as a social determinant to better health, or that it at very least provides the stable and safe environments needed to support effective healthcare practices and recovery.

Trauma and Healing Relationships

The unfortunate reality is that many of the people with complex trauma issues we serve have traditionally *not* had access to safe and stable housing. They have experienced significant layered or compound trauma ranging from childhood abuse and domestic violence to the trauma associated with becoming homeless, as well suffering the ill effects of prolonged homelessness. In addition, they often struggle with a range of mental health, addiction, and medical concerns. These vulnerable folks often take part in a broad spectrum of human services from community resource centers, meal programs, and homeless outreach services to shelters, UK Homeless Hostels or Transitional Housing programs, as well as various other types of longer-term residential settings and/or Housing First Apartments. Regardless of where we meet people, our work is dependent upon our ability to establish positive working relationships. Even during the age of Information Technology, and perhaps even more so because of it, we seek out meaningful connections. In fact, we know that healthy relationships (Seikkula, 2011; Wampold, 2001) are healing in themselves, apart from any particular form of treatment or approach to recovery. Our successful work in the field depends upon our ability to establish trusting relationships with people who have experienced compounded trauma, homelessness, and loss.

This is where Pretreatment shines! It is all about engagement and doing person-centered work with folks who are initially reluctant to take part in services. Throughout this text, we have jointly reviewed in detail the applications of a Pretreatment assessment that is based on five universal principles of care. Our focus is to build successful pretreatment pathways to safe housing, medical, mental health, and addiction care, including recovery and Peer Support services. The exercises and narrative excerpts serve the purpose of actively engaging the reader and shining a light on the integration of practice and theory. My hope is to equip human service and medical professionals, workers, and students of all stripes with the Pretreatment guidance and skills needed to improve assessment and intervention with vulnerable populations that are reticent to participate in services. The main focus is the facilitation of meaningful connections between workers and clients that can unleash the healing power of relationship-centered work. Beyond that, it is really about getting to know people's stories as we journey together in our efforts to achieve better health.

Constructing New Narratives and Pretreatment Pathways to Inclusion

My own experiences of outreach in a variety of settings, ranging from the streets of New York City to the woods and riversides of Western Massachusetts, have taught me to believe in the power of narrative. As I've stated previously in *Cross-Cultural Dialogues on Homelessness* (2018), "Telling stories is an all too human way of communication, which has served us well through the ages. We have come to understand the *Power of Myth* (Campbell, 1988), whether it be in written form or part of an oral tradition of storytelling, to help put forth and preserve our sense of culture, values and important lessons learned. The wisdom we can garner is often best communicated in the form of a story or narrative."

Throughout my own journey into human service, I have learned a great deal from Michael White's (2000) and others' writings on Narrative therapy. Epston and White (1992) state, "In striving to make sense of life, persons have the task of arranging their experiences of events in sequences across time in such a way as to arrive at a coherent account of themselves and the world around them... This account can be referred to as a story or self-narrative." They view our life journey as something that can be understood as a story and can thereby be examined and reframed by its author.

We would be wise to respect that people are the authors of their own stories (Epston & White, 1992; Freedman & Combs, 1996). We can create the opportunity for people to construct their own narratives by providing client-centered relationships that encourage people to find their voice, and thereby get perspective on their journey. Our role is to encourage Open Dialogue and foster a Common Language to spur a Being Here connection. A Being Here connection is best exemplified when both the client and worker establish a common frame of reference, sharing the same house of language, so issues can be jointly explored and new narratives can be formed, while always respecting the autonomy of the person (Levy, 2010). This invariably strengthens the client-worker relationship and future dialogue. It is through the dynamic process of a true Open Dialogue that we can begin to hear one another and consider different points of view.

Sharon Salzberg (2011, p. 177), states, "Loving-kindness is essentially a form of inclusiveness of caring, rather than categorizing others in terms of those whom we care for and those who can be easily excluded, ignored or disdained... A deepening of insight will inevitably include seeing how all of our lives are inextricably interconnected." Although our experiences and cultures may differ, we know that people are people and all of us require basic health and safety in order to thrive. As John Conolly pointed out so eloquently in his introduction, Pretreatment is a means toward greater compassion, facilitating therapeutic connections, and inclusion of the folks who have been most ignored and cast to the fringes of society. In the end, it is about the hope and purpose that positive person-centered relationships can instill on our quest to better health! This book provides the roadmap. It invites the reader, through an interactive and reflective process of exercises, examining narrative excerpts, and asking critical questions, to develop the skills, as well as embrace and apply the Pretreatment perspective necessary for us to succeed on this meaningful journey.

References

Bakhtin, M. M., (1981). translation by C. Emerson, & M. Holquist, (ed) *The Dialogic Imagination: four essays* Austin: The University of Texas Press.

Bretherton, J. & Pleace, N. (2015). *Housing first in England: An evaluation of nine services.* Center for Housing Policy: University of York

Campbell, J., with Moyers, B. (1988) *The Power of Myth.* New York, NY: MJF Books

Freedman, J. & Combs, G. (1996) *Narrative therapy: The social construction of preferred realities.* New York: W. W. Norton Company, Inc.

Levy, J. S. with Johnson, R. (2018). *Cross-cultural dialogues on homelessness: From* pretreatment strategies to psychological environments. Ann Arbor, MI: Loving Healing Press.

Levy, J. S. (2010) *Homeless narratives & pretreatment pathways: From words to housing.* Ann Arbor, MI: Loving Healing Press.

O'Connell, J. J. (2005). *Premature Mortality in Homeless Populations: A Review of the Literature,* 19 pages. Nashville: National Health Care for the Homeless Council, Inc.

O'Connell, J. J & Swain S. (2005). *Rough sleepers: A five year prospective study in Boston, 1999-2003.* Presentation, Tenth Annual Ending Homelessness Conference, Massachusetts Housing and Shelter Alliance, Waltham, MA.

O'Connell, J. J. *Vulnerability Index.* Retrieved on 8/2/17 from jedc.org web site http://www.jedc.org/forms/Vulnerability%20Index.pdf

Roncarati, J. S. (2016). Examining the Mortality of an Unsheltered Homeless Cohort From Boston, MA, 2000 Through 2009. Doctoral dissertation, Harvard T. H. Chan School of Public Health. http://nrs.harvard.edu/urn-3: HUL.InstRepos: 32644540

Salzberg, S. (2011). Mindfulness and loving-kindness, *Contemporary Buddhism*, 12:1, 177-182, DOI: 10.1080/14639947.2011.564837

Seikkula, J. (2011). Becoming Dialogical: Psychotherapy or a way of Life? *The Australian* and New Zealand Journal of Family Therapy. 32(3): 179-193

Stefancic, A. & Tsemberis, S. (2007). Housing first for long-term shelter dwellers with psychiatric disabilities in a suburban county: A four-year study of housing access and retention. *The Journal of Primary Prevention*, 28(3-4): 265-279.

Tsemberis, S. (2010). Housing First: Ending homelessness, promoting recovery and reducing cost. In I. Ellen & B. O'Flaherty (eds) *How to House the Homeless.* New York: Russell Sage Foundation.

Wampold, B. E. (2001). *The great psychotherapy Debate: Models, methods, findings.* Mahwah, New Jersey: Lawrence Erlbaum Associates.

White M. (2000). *Reflections on Narrative Practice: Essays and Interviews.* Adelaide: Dulwich Centre Publications.

About the Authors

Jay S. Levy, MSW, LICSW — Clinical Social Worker, PATH Program Manager, Teacher

Jay S. Levy has spent more than thirty years working with individuals who experience homelessness. He is the author of the highly acclaimed book *Pretreatment Guide for Homeless Outreach & Housing First*. Jay's 2018 project was a collaborative effort with several authors from the UK. It is entitled *Cross-Cultural Dialogues on Homelessness: From Pretreatment Strategies to Psychologically Informed Environments*. He has also published a monograph and several journal articles on Homelessness issues.

He developed Pretreatment as an approach for helping people without homes who are often deemed "not ready" and excluded from housing and/or recovery-oriented services and treatment. He has helped to create new Housing First programs such as the Regional Engagement and Assessment for Chronically Homeless program (REACH).

Jay is currently employed by Eliot CHS-Homeless Services as a Regional Manager for the statewide SAMHSA-PATH Homeless Outreach Team. As an adjunct teacher at Anna Maria College, he recently taught a unique graduate psychology course on Outreach Counseling, which integrated Pretreatment and PIE perspectives with the clinical challenges of homeless services work.

He has achieved formal recognition from the Commonwealth of Massachusetts Department of Mental Health for his ongoing efforts to help under-served homeless individuals through his direct service, clinical supervision of staff, and program development. Jay received his MSW degree in clinical social work from Columbia University in 1988.

Jay lives in Western MA with his wife, Louise, who teaches science at a local high school. His two children, Talia and Sara, have both graduated college and have begun their initial journeys into career-related activities. More information on Jay and his work can be found at www.jayslevy.com.

John Conolly, UKCP reg. Psychotherapist, Lacanian Analyst, M.A. (Psychoanalysis), M.A. (Psychology)

John practiced many years as an Organisational Psychologist before becoming a Lacanian Analyst and Psychotherapist. His interest in the interface between individual self-exclusion and organisational marginalisation processes led him to his present role as "Service Lead" for the Westminster Homeless Health Counselling Service, at the CLCH NHS Trust, London. He also took on the role of (honorary) Chair for the Camden and Islington Foundation NHS Trust, Recovery College in 2019.

He is also a Pathway Clinical Fellow, and a Member of the Council for Psychoanalysis and Jungian Analysis College, and a Member of the Centre for Freudian Analysis and Research. He is a United Kingdom Council for Psychotherapy (UKCP) registered Psychoanalytic Psychotherapist, and Lacanian Analyst. He has taught at the Tavistock and Portman NHS Trust, as well as at the Middlesex University, Mental Health Department.

John founded the Westminster *Complex Personalities* network in 2010, and has spoken extensively at conferences and authored several chapters on *Pre-treatment Therapy,* an attachment, trauma informed, buildings based, counseling approach he developed, based on Jay Levy's "Pretreatment" outreach model for engaging and supporting homeless people in the USA, and which is increasingly drawing attention, nationally and internationally.

He recently developed a popular *Trauma Informed Communications Skills* training program and is presently working on a book entitled *Stories from the Basement — A Psychotherapist's Reflections on Caring for Homeless People and the Obstacles to Compassion.*

John lives in north London with his wife, two daughters, their cat and dog.

Joel Hunt, MPAS, PA-C, Street Medicine Director, Physician Assistant, Teacher

Joel Hunt has over thirteen years of delivering healthcare to people experiencing homelessness. He graduated from the University of Utah where he received a Masters of Physician Assistant Studies after serving six years in the US Army. Joel began his career in medicine with people experiencing homelessness in Salt Lake City, Utah at 4th Street Clinic, a Health Care for the Homeless grantee and Federally Qualified Health Clinic where he started a street medicine program. Joel later moved to Fort Worth, Texas to help establish street medicine in Tarrant County at the publicly funded JPS Health Network where he continues to work for Acclaim Physician Group, a partner with JPS Health Network.

He has been responsible for oversight and implementation of the Street Medicine team, collaborating with community partners for development of services such as integrating housing and healthcare, recuperative care, healthcare and homelessness research, and resident physician and student training opportunities in street medicine including a family medicine street medicine track and street medicine fellowship.

Joel's goal is to bring healthcare to people experiencing homelessness, improve health outcomes, reduce suffering, and promote dignity and equality resulting in a positive community impact.

Index

Pretreatment Guide for Homeless Outreach & Housing First

This book provides social workers, outreach clinicians, case managers, and concerned community members with a pretreatment guide for assisting homeless couples, youth, and single adults. The inter-relationship between Homeless Outreach and Housing First is examined in detail to inform program development and hands on practice. *Pretreatment Guide for Homeless Outreach & Housing First* shares five detailed case studies from the field to elucidate effective ways of helping and to demonstrate how the most vulnerable among us can overcome trauma and homelessness. Readers will:

- Expand their assessment skills and discover new interventions for helping people who have experienced long-term or chronic homelessness.

- Understand and be able to integrate the stages of common language construction with their own practice.

- Learn about the positive measurable impact of a Housing First approach and its moral, fiscal, and quality of life implications.

- Understand how to better integrate program policy and supervision with Homeless Outreach & Housing First initiatives.

- Learn how to utilize a Pretreatment Approach with couples, youth, and unaccompanied adults experiencing untreated major mental illness and addiction.

"Jay S. Levy's book is essential reading to both people new to the movement to end homelessness and folks who have been in the trenches for many years. Learn how to do effective outreach with the chronic homeless population, and the ins and outs of the Housing First model. The personal stories and the success cases will give inspiration to work even harder to help both individuals and for ending homelessness in your community."

Michael Stoops, Director of Community Organizing
National Coalition for the Homeless, Washington, DC

ISBN 978-1-61599-201-0
From Loving Healing Press

Cross-Cultural Dialogues on Homelessness Reveal New Insights

This groundbreaking book presents compelling narratives and innovative approaches for addressing the psychological traumas that can underlie homelessness and is the first to explore in-depth what the US and UK can learn from one another.

Authors focus on understanding and applying the precepts of Pretreatment and "Psychologically Informed Environments," as well as effective ways to promote productive dialogue on all levels -- with clients, clinicians, advocates, policymakers, researchers, and others. Detailed case studies review and integrate "hands on" practice with Appreciative Inquiry, Open Dialogue, and Common Language Construction methods.

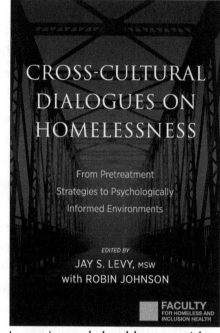

"In *Cross-Cultural Dialogues on Homelessness*, Jay Levy and co-authors provide the conceptual tools, the hitherto 'missing language', needed by practitioners and policymakers working with excluded individuals. This book has been informed by the authors' practice and should come with a warning: it will revolutionise how you work -- irreversibly and, undoubtedly, for the better"

-- Cliona Ni Cheallaigh, MB, MRCP, PhD, Senior Lecturer in Medical Gerontology,
  Trinity College (Dublin)

"Jay distills many decades of his own street experience, and by cross comparing his brilliant schema of Pretreatment with the British model of Psychologically Informed Environments (PIE), he reveals the underlying common processes of effective street engagement. As a long-time practitioner of street medicine, I recommend this book to anyone who seeks that sacred place on the streets where healing begins."

-- Jim Withers, MD, Founder and Medical Director and Operation Safety Net
  and the Street Medicine Institute (Pittsburgh)

ISBN 978-1-61599-366-6
From Loving Healing Press

Notes

CPSIA information can be obtained
at www.ICGtesting.com
Printed in the USA
BVHW050357141021
618855BV00012B/647